MAKE YOURSELVES READY

VOLUME ONE

Part One of a Teaching Manual on
Casting Out Demons for Christians

PETER HOBSON

"And by Salvation, I mean not merely deliverance from hell, but a present deliverance from sin, a RESTORATION of the soul to its primitive health, a recovery of the Divine Nature."

John Wesley in
"Farther Appeal to Men of Reason and Religion".

MAKE YOURSELVES READY
Book 1 of the Christian Deliverance Series
by Peter and Verlie Hobson
Copyright ©1988

FULL SALVATION FELLOWSHIP
ISBN: 0947252010

Quotations from The New Testament are generally my own translation, otherwise I have usually used The Revised Standard Version of the Bible.

CHRISTIAN DELIVERANCE PREFACE

This series [produced in four (4) parts] is addressed to Christian soldiers for two main reasons. It is hoped that it will assist responsible Christians in the exercise of the ministry of deliverance within their assemblies, and also impart a new level of understanding and maturity to those who seek more and more to walk in the Spirit as soldiers of Christ Jesus. The format has been designed as a course for the purpose of training deacons, counselors, potential Church leaders and, indeed, any Christian who feels led to be informed and/or serve in this particular area of spiritual warfare.

Much of the material is revelational in that the ministry of deliverance is itself a revelational ministry because when we cast out demons by the Spirit of God, then the Kingdom of God comes upon us. The ministry wages war in the realm of the spirit-world and overthrows strongholds of deception and ignorance and, when this happens, it is like scales being removed from our eyes, enabling us to "see" things previously hidden from us.

There will be some Christians who will think it a mistake to publish a book of this nature, believing that the misuse of its information may create dangerous situations, but the fact of the matter is that television screens and secular bookshops are FULL of dangerous UNCLEAN (occult, sexual and violent) material and people everywhere are playing with fire — some aware — some unaware — of the frightful spiritual danger to which they expose themselves. Warfare always carries an element of danger, and this is no time to be faint-hearted.

It is too late in God's timetable to hold back the truth any longer. God's revelation and solution must be made known as a matter of urgency. The time is short.

The world is in big trouble and Jesus is coming soon for a beautiful bride – the Universal Church. Unfortunately, if He came today, He would be marrying a very troubled, divided, unclean lady — more like a mixed-up, ugly hag. It is God's time for the big clean-up. The Bride must make herself ready. She is already clothed with the righteous clothing of Jesus on the outside, being justified by faith, but NOW is the time for her cleansing in the inward parts. NOW is the full and great Salvation of our God ready to be revealed, that the Bride might truly be without spot or blemish for her Lord.

Peter Hobson
Crows Nest, Sydney, N.S.W.
January, 1985

Addition to the Preface

October 1991

If you bought and read an earlier edition of this book and thought it was very good, even invaluable, I would have to agree with you. I boast in the Lord because I know Who is responsible for all this revelational material.

However I strongly recommend that you give your old copy to some other interested Christian and buy this one for your further study.

Vital subjects, such as an examination of the Victory of the Cross and seven (7) foundations for a deliverance ministry make it one of the most powerful books of its kind in print anywhere — all glory to the Lord Jesus Christ.

And when you have studied and been blessed, share it with someone else. May the good Lord set you on fire with His full salvation and mightily use you.

Peter H.

SCRIPTURAL ENCOURAGEMENT FOR READING THIS BOOK:

"My people are destroyed for lack of knowledge" says the Lord.

Hosea 4:6

"The scripture on which I spoke was this (is it possible anyone should be ignorant that it is **fulfilled in every true minister of Christ?**): The Spirit of the Lord is upon me, because He hath anointed me to preach the gospel to the poor; He hath sent me to heal the broken-hearted, to preach deliverance to the captives, and recovering of sight to the blind, to set at liberty them that are bruised, to proclaim the acceptable year of the Lord."

John Wesley's Journal – 2nd April, 1739.

"If you continue in My word, you are truly My disciples, and **you will know the truth, and the truth will make you free**."

Jesus Christ – John 8:31–32

"**The Lord has more truth** and light yet to break forth out of His Holy Word."

John Robinson - "Mayflower" – 1620.

"Let us find the **truth!**"

John Calvin – c. 1534.

"Jesus Christ is the same, yesterday, today and forever."

Hebrews 13:8

"For God did not appoint us for wrath, but to **obtain salvation** through our Lord Jesus Christ."

1 Thessalonians 5:9

BOOKS BY PETER HOBSON

Published by FULL SALVATION FELLOWSHIP LTD

MENTAL ILLNESS - WHAT CAN CHRISTIANS DO?

CHRISTIAN DELIVERANCE BOOK 1 -
MAKE YOURSELVES READY

CHRISTIAN DELIVERANCE BOOK 2 -
ENGAGING THE ENEMY

CHRISTIAN DELIVERANCE BOOK 3 -
WALKING IN VICTORY

CHRISTIAN DELIVERANCE BOOK 4 -
WE ALL HAVE OUR DEMONS

GUIDANCE FOR THOSE RECEIVING DELIVERANCE

HEADCOVERING AND LADY PASTOR-TEACHERS

CHRISTIAN AUTHORITY AND POWER & THE STIGMATA

END-TIME DELIVERANCE & THE HOLY SPIRIT REVIVAL
(3RD ED.)

YOUR FULL SALVATION IN CHRIST JESUS

SURVIVING THE DISTRESS OF NATIONS

TORONTO AND THE TRUTHS YOU NEED TO KNOW

SEX, DEMONS AND MORALITY

RELIGIOUS SPIRITS

BEWARE HYPOCRISY

See our Website **www.fullsalvationfellowship.com.au**
for worldwide commendations

CONTENTS

INTRODUCTION

These are studies in what has come to be known as the Deliverance Ministry and I would like to warn the Christian reader about a few things first before we even start. Obviously the viewpoints expressed are my own and I alone must take responsibility for them and nobody else. I think it is safe to say that many things I share with you will cut across what you already believe. I don't think it is going to make any difference whether you are of a Pentecostal stream or of a historic conservative stream of church tradition, I am almost sure to cut across some of the things that you hold dear at the present time, and I trust that you will be patient with me and examine the things that I am suggesting for their own value and not because of anything else. I don't claim to be an expert in this Ministry. I don't think anybody at any time can be an expert before God because we are very conscious of the measure of the grace of God for each one of us and that everything we have is given by God for each one of us to share with the Body of Christ as we are led, and we thank Him for that. So I am not coming before you as a know-all but I believe that the Word of God which I am going to share with you will carry its own convictions and authority.

However, I do ask you to **have an open mind and teachable heart in every direction**; that is very important, of course. Much of what follows in this introduction to the ministry of deliverance may be breaking new ground for many Christian leaders. I stress that it is an introduction only and would remind readers that **a correct diagnosis is essential** before a right course can be adopted to bring about a Godly solution. Our aim is to give

Christian soldiers practical advice from the Scriptures and our experience in order to enable them to enter into the victory which Christ has already obtained for them, rather like the children of Israel entering into battle for the Promised Land which God had already declared belonged to them (Joshua 1:3). The victory is ours by God's Word, but we have to go to war against the forces of darkness for it to become real in our experience. In other words, **we must act on the Word that God has spoken.**

Some essentials of Christianity have always had two sides to the fulfillment of God's Word. There is the *LEGAL, COVENANTAL* side of the covenant of God which has been achieved in point of time by Jesus Christ the Son of God, on Calvary's Cross; and there is the EXPERIENTIAL side where that which is legally the Christian's becomes his or hers in experience. Christ died for our sins and, legally, a new covenant has been established between God and man, made in God's image. It is by **GRACE** through **FAITH** we are saved for eternal life, and whereas Christ was victor and satan vanquished on that Cross, one doesn't *EXPERIENCE* that victory (simply by "faith" in Christ) UNTIL one is sealed by the Holy Spirit for "**anyone who does not have the Spirit of Christ does not belong to Him**" (Romans 8:9). Likewise in the area of healing, or deliverance from satan, faith in what Christ has accomplished for us at a point of time in history must be exercised in the present time of need, and will still require the seal and operation of the Spirit in response to our faith, in order for us to **experience** victory.

That is why Joshua and the Israelites still needed to invade the Promised Land in battle formation — already theirs by the Word and Promise of God. The battles had to be fought for what was already theirs by right (God's authority). Likewise, we also need to use by faith that which God has provided in His New Covenant if we are to obtain the benefits and victories that the Covenant offers. **The enemies of God are just as reluctant to acknowledge their defeat today as they were in Joshua's time.** Please read that last sentence again. It is one of the KEYS for winning spiritual warfare.

In one sense God has spoken. It is past — it is done — it is written, and in another sense we still have to play the part of the Christian soldier, taking up our divine weapons for the tearing down of strongholds in spiritual warfare. Our legal rights have been obtained; now we have to experience them.

Thus we ignore the Ministry of Deliverance at our peril, because it is a genuine ministry provided by the New Covenant for the Church of Christ and for the day in which we live.

In rediscovering the Ministry of Deliverance in this dynamic twentieth century, we have one unusual advantage in that there are very few inflexible traditions of men with which to wrestle in order to establish a biblical pattern of ministry. We may go direct to the Holy Scriptures for our guidelines generally uncluttered by the ritualism of men in other ages.

HOW WE STARTED

Well, very simply I came into the Healing Ministry in 1964 through the testimony of a devout young businessman, Mr. Adrian Martens, who quickly demolished all my objections, after I experienced some initial uneasiness.

I had been so grounded by my theological training to trust God's Word even when all the evidence of experience was in conflict, that I knew it was not the Word of God that failed but my own lack of spiritual understanding.

The Lord was gracious to encourage me with several minor healings within my family — some of them were remarkably instantaneous so that even through experience I knew I was on the right track.

However, I realised very early that if we were going to continue progressing in the Healing Ministry, sooner or later, we would have to face demons. The New Testament is full of such clashes and there was no way that I could see being able to avoid this development. This was a time of serious wrestling in the Spirit for me because I didn't particularly want to go in that direction of ministry. I was happy about the healing direction but not about the demonic direction. But we all have to wrestle with these things in our ongoing Christian walk and the Lord really gave me Hobson's Choice,[1] in the matter, so we went on.

I remember a case of a Public Servant who was in a position of counseling people and making decisions for troubled families in great need and he came to me one day and said, "Oh, I have had a breakdown. I have had to leave. I have to have a break from the job". He said, "And I can't cope. I'm always having to make decisions for families, terrible rending decisions forced upon me in my job, and I just can't stand it. I can't cope with it any more". It was obvious to anyone that he was full of spirits of fear and despair. So I sat him across the vestry table in St. Stephens, Penrith and put a Bible on the table between us (I had read somewhere that someone else had taken that precaution when beginning deliverance work and I was taking no chances). When I look back on it now and see what a puerile act that was, thinking that the book itself would protect me, rather than the spoken, living Word of authority through a disciple of Christ operating under the leading of the Holy Spirit, I am obliged to laugh at myself, but it seemed a good idea at the time. Then I began to minister, "Come out in Jesus' Name!"

I hammered away for a while and got absolutely nothing as far as I could see — no reaction or manifestations whatsoever — and after a while he looked up with rather sad eyes and asked me, "Have you done this before?" I didn't want to tell him that I hadn't because I thought he might lose heart, so I avoided the question by referring to the Bible, as much for my own encouragement as

1 No choice at all, according to English Literature.

his. He was my first real crack at the deliverance ministry and we really got nowhere — I am terribly sorry to have to say that. But you know what it is like when the Lord is in something; you can't really hold back, and He makes you go on, even if things don't work out the first time.

I was convinced about the activity of demons by this time (1969) and my wife Verlie was saying, "Oh, you and your demons. You are always talking about demons". Anyway, shortly after that — about two weeks later — she was called by phone to visit a parishioner in distress. It turned out to be a heavy smoker fighting desperately to quit, and for whom Verlie offered some fervent prayer. There was quite a dramatic deliverance with hammer-like explosions in the head and chunks of nicotine being coughed up. This was an important breakthrough for both of us; a breakthrough for Verlie to be used that way when she had serious doubts, and a breakthrough for me because at last something had happened — and a victory at that.

There was a three-year break in which we were encouraged by a few healings, and the matter of deliverance was mentally pigeon-holed for future use, God willing.

I had been guided into Ordination by the Lord through the gift of prophecy ministered by prophetesses und er the headship of **Rev. Barry Schofield**, the Anglican Rector of the parish of Picton, N.S.W. During a curacy at Eastwood parish I received an invitation to take a run-down inner Sydney parish, and while seeking the Lord on the matter, received a prophecy through the Picton ministry on August 17, 1971:

"My son, I have told you I would lead and guide and bless you. This is my Spirit's leading. Go ahead and I will be your strength, your wisdom and your understanding. This will be a hard job but you are the man I have chosen to do this work for me. Your wife, too, will help much in this work. Although this will be hard there will be much blessing come out of it eventually. Go in the strength of your Lord."

A few weeks later a Word of knowledge came through another ministry:

"I know my son. I have a great work for him (P.H.) to do."

This was followed by a Holy Spirit Seminar on November 6th, 1971. Again the Lord spoke through prophecy:

"The Lord is sending you to a new place, a new dimension of life you haven't known. You will be anointed in a way you haven't known before. Do not rely on yourself, but the Lord. Great work will be done. The Spirit will move as never before (and) will bring you out of uncertainty into light."

This was followed some months later with a *Word of knowledge* through the Picton ministry:

"My purpose is being worked out. There will come a time when he (P.H.) can speak LOUDLY. Much blessing will come if he waits MY time."

I certainly needed that last piece of advice about waiting. (The Lord had already told me through a Word in 1967 that I was impatient, headstrong and slow to understand).

Then came the next stepping-stone — completely unexpected. Arriving at St. Michael's Church, Surry Hills in 1972, we had a young man cleaning the church who had been rejected for ordination in the Church of England in Australia because he had epilepsy. While I was in the vestry one Saturday morning, he was cleaning the choir stalls and I heard a terrible scream, followed by a crash of furniture. Rushing out of the vestry, I found him underneath the pews, thrashing around and experiencing another epileptic attack. Well, of course, this really frightened me and so with nothing else that I could do and all alone (and I can see God's hand in this) I verbally lashed into the spirit of epilepsy in Jesus' Name — not only because I believed I was able but because I was afraid and desperate, and there was no alternative help or ministry available. He recovered in about five or ten minutes and we helped him out to the car and took him home. Later on I learned that he had applied for Ordination in another Diocese and insisted on being tested again by the doctors involved. To everyone's delight he was found to be virtually free of any signs of his affliction. There was just the faintest touch on his test results that he had had epilepsy and so he was accepted for the work which was his heart's desire, praise the Lord, and that was a tremendous step forward for us also. He now has a wonderful teaching and healing ministry all over the world.

In 1973 we entered into a ministry against the spirit of fear with a full-time Deaconess, a dedicated Christian, and we discovered that a person can have more than one spirit and need more than one deliverance session. She had asked for prayer with the *laying on of hands* for several weeks but I had declined because she couldn't give me any reason or purpose to pray for. She finally said, "I don't know. I just feel unsettled and would like you to pray for me". I don't like laying hands on anyone suddenly, but finally agreed rather uneasily to her request. With a theological student's help we sat the lass in a chair in my study and began to pray for the Lord's blessing on her. Glancing down I saw, to my horror, her face contorting just as I was about to close the prayer. Seeing her condition I kept on praying, but the more I prayed the worse she looked. Suddenly I caught on, and cried out, **"Come out in Jesus' Name!"** At the fourth consecutive command, there was a sudden physical release, from all the physical tension and facial contortion, and a flood of tears briefly. The student[1] was standing by open-mouthed. "I didn't expect that," he said. "I thought you

1 Later Principal of a Missionary College.

were going to pray a little prayer asking for God's help for her." "So did I," I replied. Three months later she was still manifesting or exhibiting the same problems and so we tackled her again, but this time kept the ministry going after the first release, eventually casting out eleven spirits of fear before the manifestations ceased. *This experience very effectively taught us not to cease ministry after one release and send the person away under the false illusion that they were "healed".* We also learned never to claim total healing or deliverance, for only God is in a position to know that, and the subject will know soon enough whether he or she is entirely free or not — let THEM make the claims and give glory to God for what He has done through faith in Christ. And — most importantly — **I learned that Christians — even Bible-trained "professionals" — could be demonised.**

In October, 1973, a fourth-year medical student was referred to us for help. Soundly converted, his Christian growth was nil, due to involvement with various drugs, the Divine Light Mission (Guru), and tendencies towards homosexuality and pederasty. He experienced some wonderful deliverances and eventually left us to go back and continue his medical studies, having previously been in a serious mental state of depression and "dropping out".

This really opened the floodgates, especially as the film "The Exorcist" came to be shown in Sydney at that time. The media caught on to what was happening at St. Michael's Church, Surry Hills, and cries for help came from every part of N.S.W., indeed Australia, and we just thank God and give Him all the praise and the glory. The volume of work steadily increased, but the Lord supplied more helpers for this ministry over the years and that enabled us to cope with the volume that we faced.

To cut a long, rather messy story short, we were obliged to move out of the historic church framework so that the work could develop unfettered by church tradition, and then both my wife and I were convicted that we ourselves needed deliverance ministry if we were to continue growing in effectiveness. We received this ministry, praise the Lord!

After two years or so of cleansing, I was led back into helping one here and one there and today my wife and I operate more as a MINISTRY rather than a normal church, although all the benefits (i.e. blessings) of a normal church are available to those who have no other church home.

We do not desire to intrude into anyone's church affiliation or loyalties, and we are quite happy to minister to the needs of the Body of Christ and send people back to their assemblies in better (spiritual) shape than when they arrived.

In conclusion, **I offer to debate publicly or discuss privately these issues with any leader** who invites me to come at his or her expense, subject to the Lord's overruling and current ministry programs and obligations, of course. So if you know of any Christian leader who is beginning to move into the ministry of deliverance, do please draw their attention to this book. If they are a true man or woman of God, they will be grateful and thank the Lord (and you) for it.

Now our calling and Vision is to see the whole of the Body of Christ across the world catch fire with the **purifying and cleansing refinement of the Lord**, through the ministry of CHRISTIAN DELIVERANCE!

1

UNDERSTANDING THE PROBLEM

1. CLARIFYING OF TERMS.

All Christian readers will need a fundamental understanding of key biblical terms, as follows:

(i) Antichrist.

The term "antichrist" (1 John 4:1–6) does not necessarily mean, as so many people think, against Christ, but has a much broader application meaning instead of Christ. There are many spirits in this world today who will give some position of esteem to Jesus (always falling far short of the fact that He is THE Son of God who came in the flesh and will come again) but always present a substitute for Jesus. These might be Krishna or Maharaj Ji Guru or some other modern self-styled Christ. Jesus is tolerated but no longer as Lord for a new form of Christ has appeared, they say. Thus the word "antichrist" does not necessarily reveal a naked, visible, hostile enemy in a face-to-face encounter, but is very often a masked, surreptitious, tolerant and seemingly friendly **alternative**, the key word being "**alternative**". Anything that takes the place of Jesus Christ in a man or woman's life is an alternative and is thus antichrist. Such alternative may often be helpful to our community such as political involvement or good works but they become antichrist regardless of their respectable, even commendable, exterior — for the person who puts them in the place of Christ and to the extent that they become our religion and our reason for living.

Occult practices, of course, place no emphasis on the death and resurrection of our Lord Jesus Christ and therefore may be said to be **that part of antichrist which thrives on interest in the supernatural.**

(ii) Exorcism

Exorcism is a term which should be dropped from Christian usage except when applied to **non-Christian** deliverance. It is only used twice in the New Testament and each time by the unregenerate, viz:

(a) The Jewish itinerant exorcists who fail miserably to heal a man, using Jesus' Name but without themselves being children of God with authority (Acts 19:13).

(b) The words of adjuration by the High Priest to Jesus during His infamous "trial" by the Sanhedrin, "I adjure (exorcise) you by the living God, tell us if you are the Christ, the Son of God" (Matt. 26:63).

These give us something of the true meaning of the word — "to swear or affirm by an oath, to administer an oath to, to adjure". Therefore, we strongly deny that "exorcism" is a suitable term for describing Christian deliverance from the powers of darkness, but is perhaps more appropriate for non-Christian activity such as that of tribal witch-doctors or modern mediums or occultists **who obtain the cooperation of spirits by appeasement and sacrifices etc.** rather than removal by the authoritative proclamation of the victory of Christ.

Having said that, however, we need to be aware that occultists will use any name, even the Name of Jesus, to obtain the results they seek from the powers of darkness; but although they may obtain some results, there is a wealth of difference between those who know the Lord and use His Name for His glory and those who use His Name to cast out demons — but of whom He says, "I NEVER KNEW YOU: depart from me, you workers of iniquity!" (Matt. 7:23).

Anyone, believers or unbelievers can speak a name, and sometimes the use of the name will obtain the desired result in the same way that spiritual laws can be used by ungodly men in order to reap a material benefit, but such temporal success counts for nothing when we are one day obliged to give an account of ourselves before the Throne of Christ.

The distinction between pagan/occult exorcism or even as practised by the first-century Jews themselves (Acts 19:13, Matt. 12:27) and Christian deliverance is vitally important. This can best be illustrated by the incident in the synagogue early in Jesus' earthly ministry:

> "And the unclean spirit, convulsing him and crying with a loud voice, came out of him. And they were all amazed, so that they questioned among themselves, saying, 'What is this? A new teaching! WITH AUTHORITY HE COMMANDS EVEN THE UNCLEAN SPIRITS AND THEY OBEY HIM:' And at once His fame spread everywhere throughout all the surrounding region of Galilee."
>
> Mark 1:26–28

Jesus did not appease like the Jewish exorcists — He commanded. If the church cannot make the important distinction between occult exorcism and Christian deliverance, it is difficult to see how we can expect the world to do so. One is of God — the other is not.

(iii) Deliverance (Casting Out of Demons).

The ministry of deliverance, more popularly but unfortunately known as exorcism, is an answer for those who have been involved with antichrist at some disturbing level — but who now having turned to Jesus, seek to be free of every weight and chain cast around them in the past. **It is basic in the training of the disciples** (Matt. 10:1) **and is to be carried forward until the close of the New Testament age** (Matt. 28:20). Indeed it is to be observed (i.e. kept strictly, guarded, preserved) by the disciples of all nations and all generations until Christ's return, and it is difficult to see how any pastor or Christian can deny its relevance for today unless he also deny the relevance of the Great Commission of Jesus Christ to His Church as recorded in Matthew.[1] It is unfortunately true that some pastors today know more about the synoptic problem of the New Testament or the J.E.D. and P. redactic problem[2] of the Old Testament, but **the ministry of deliverance is a New Testament commission from Christ** and it is there for all those who are convinced of the truth of God's Word and its relevance to their faith.

"Deliverance" is the most common term used by Christians when referring to casting out demons or unclean spirits, and derives from the Lord's prayer, "… and lead us not into temptation BUT DELIVER US FROM EVIL or THE EVIL ONE". It is therefore a scriptural term and much easier to use than the longer but more common biblical term "casting out demons". "Deliver" has a sense of rescuing and can be literally translated, "But rescue us from evil (or, the evil one)."

That is rather beautiful, isn't it? It is not difficult to see from this

---

1 The authority to cast out demons and heal every disease, and the command to carry forward that authority and ministry throughout the New Testament Age is of such importance to every obedient Christian as to warrant the strongest emphasis. It is discussed more fully in Book 3.

2 A theory pertaining to the authorship of the first five books of the Bible.

why the man who had the Legion is described as being "saved" in the gospel of Luke the physician (8:36). It should be obvious that rescuing, delivering, saving, are simply different words describing the Saviourhood of our Lord Jesus Christ. It is an exercise of the saving power of the gospel. It is not an addition to the gospel — it is not a by-product of the gospel — **but it is an integral part of the gospel.** It is true that nothing can replace the salvation of the human spirit as the most important salvation that the Lord offers His creation but it also ought to be clear that **opposition to Christ's deliverance is opposition to the saving grace of the gospel of our Lord Jesus Christ** because He is the great Deliverer of our souls and the great Healer of our bodies (flesh). Thus spirit, soul and body are saved by Him when believers appropriate His FULL SALVATION.

(iv) Spirit.

What is a spirit (with a small "s")? We know that the Old Testament Hebrew word "*ruach*" can be translated wind, breath or spirit, and that the New Testament Greek word "*pneuma*" can also mean wind or spirit. When God made man He breathed his **(man's) spirit** into him and he became a living soul. **God's angels** are described as ministering spirits and **satan's demons are described as unclean spirits, while demons themselves have spirits** (Luke 4:33, Rev. 16:14).

The Holy Spirit is compared to the wind by Jesus (John 3:8) and is the person of the Godhead who energises God's purposes and executes His will in Jesus' Name. It is interesting to note that (i) the **Holy Spirit** moves like a wind and (ii) **man's spirit** leaves him at death, sometimes like a gasp of breath as when Jesus uttered a cry and yielded up His spirit (Matt. 27:50).

The obvious activity of **unclean spirits** can sometimes be discerned by an icy-cold atmosphere (contrary to expectations) or from within a person by symptoms of halitosis or body odour, but of course there are many other ways of discerning the presence of spirits which are discussed later. Perhaps I ought to explain here very quickly that confronting a demon "spirit" is, as a rule, nothing like the kind of spiritual clash that you find with the film "The Exorcist" or in the book. Now, I don't doubt that they were a reasonably true rendition of that incident, but it was a very severe one indeed. MOST of the unclean spirits coming against us (Christians) are not very strong. Have the faith of God (Mark 11:22). Have the faith of the Son of God (Gal. 2:20 lit.).

I understand that a "spirit" is a breath or a wind with personality. The Holy Spirit of God is the Holy Breath of God (Ezek. 37:9, John 20:22). At death the human spirit leaves the body as a breath (reversing Genesis 2:7) and the substance of an unclean spirit is also a breath. This explains why so many leave the human body as yawns or coughs or sneezes. They are expelled; thrust out as breaths in the same way that the body throws out poisonous waste products such as carbon dioxide.

Just as food for thought, it is interesting to note that when a person sneezes, friends close by will often remark, "Bless you!" This is simply short for "God bless you!" — and indeed it is a blessing from God that we do often **sneeze** out the foul creatures. Likewise when we **yawn** in church it does not necessarily mean the sermon or service is dull or lacking. Indeed it could mean quite the reverse[1]. When one begins to manifest unclean spirits and they queue up to leave, they very often induce a state of physical tiredness and heaviness — even sleep — in an attempt to stop the Holy Spirit achieving too much. The yawns may seem to flow from sleepiness, but they may simply be due to a spiritual "pileup" in the body with weak spirits spilling out from whatever avenue is available to them. Going under the power of God is very common today — no drama, but rather peaceful!

---

1 Some have questioned this statement, but our message tapes can prove it. Deliverance sounds in the background are unmistakable.

Likewise, that irritating **coughing** during a sermon — don't complain but praise the Lord that His Word is not appreciated by the powers of darkness — even if unbeknown to the afflicted subject. Get used to them leaving your listeners while you preach, and inwardly rejoice.

(v) Manifestation.

This is a word that is used to describe the WAY an unclean spirit reveals its presence, or its departure. As well as the yawns, coughs and sneezes mentioned above, other manifestations evidencing the removal of unclean spirits can be retching, aches and pains throughout the body (especially in the hands, legs or feet), sweating, shuddering followed by limpness, eyes watering, or just pressure lifting from the top of the head, etc.

A clergyman friend of mine whom I know has been getting closer and closer to the Lord since his "retirement" (he is actually busier than ever for the Lord these days) told me recently that he seemed to be suffering from dyspepsia (continual burping) which made him think he had some kind of infirmity.

My mind immediately flashed to **Martin Luther**, the great German reformer of the 16th century who also was believed to have suffered from dyspepsia. One film on his life story depicted him belching quite coarsely, yet this was the man who grew very close to God, especially as he translated the scriptures into German. Any translator of the scriptures will tell you that such work is a uniquely enriching experience — you can almost hear the mind of God tick over in your own spirit as you ponder each word.

I have been convinced for some time that Luther did not suffer from dyspepsia as such, but was simply receiving some **cleansing deliverance** as he drew closer to God, unbeknown to him or anyone else, and I shared this with my brother in Christ. Whether I convinced him or not remains to be seen!

For the cynics who scoff at anything outside of their own experience and intellectual knowledge, perhaps I should add that I also experienced dyspepsia soon after I began ministering deliverance to others on a regular basis back in 1974. At the time I could not understand it and it was years before I realised that in ministering spiritual cleansing to others, I myself was getting ministry also. Praise the Name of the Lord!

Sufferers receiving **the blessing of regular deliverance** week by week will often feel **bloated** during the days following ministry. This is nothing to worry about — simply the collection of spiritual pollution in the stomach or bowels prior to evacuation. The discomfort is only temporary, and like all other symptoms, is really a cause for praising the Lord.

If you are one of those people who believe that Aborigines and adherents of other non-Christian religions often know more about spiritual warfare than "educated" westerners, the following report from China by John Amy may interest you:

> The Chinese trains are surprisingly good. However, you should opt for "soft" class sleepers — four-berth compartments virtually reserved for decadent Westerners and high party officials. The "hard" class accommodation is not nearly as salubrious, and the local habit of continually spitting to rid the system of evil spirits can prove a shock for the uninitiated.[1]

It sounds strange, doesn't it? I cannot speak for the Chinese, but we had a dear brother who travelled 150 Kms to come to our Deliverance and Restoration meeting every Sunday — by train. He once complained to me that after the meeting he was obliged to spit all the 150 Kms travelling home, which he found very embarrassing. However he persevered and, praise God, he is through that now and witnessing to a full salvation wherever he goes.

1 Sydney Morning Herald - March 1987.

(a) Absence of Manifestations.

You may have the impression that everybody has quite marked and magnificent manifestations during the Ministry of Deliverance, but quite a lot of people don't appear to manifest at all during the ministry and it doesn't seem to make any difference to the results they obtain[1]. The folk who simply allow us to pray for them, although they may not manifest any kind of expulsion whatsoever, nevertheless seem to improve just as quickly as the others. There doesn't *have* to be an obvious manifestation, but many spirits are weak and being invisible, they will leave without any obvious sign of them leaving. Of course, the proof of the worth of this ministry is the actual result of well-being that the subjects receive. It may take a little time but if your subjects are finding themselves free and able to overcome certain obstacles now, perhaps caused by fears in the past, they must be improving, e.g. if they are able to talk to their boss in a less nervous way than they were able to do so before, then quite obviously the ministry is having its invisible effect and we thank God for that.

Now, 27 years later, the good Lord has made receiving deliverance a lot easier by supplying the Power of God. Breakthroughs came with the <u>Toronto Blessing</u> in 1992, and later at <u>Pensacola</u>. Because spiritual warfare was so rarely manifested in the Western traditional churches, most people did not know how to interpret all the manifestations —some were of the Holy Spirit and some were demonic, but today at the beginning of a Deliverance and Restoration meeting we use our authority and command every unclean spirit named to leave God's people quickly, quietly, and harmlessly, causing no pain, distress or discomfort whatsoever. **I strongly recommend you get a copy of our publication "Toronto and the Truths You Need to Know"!**

Early in the meeting most of the attendees feel the Power of God come upon them and head for the carpet. They receive what

---

1 Book 3 Chap. 8, 1 (iii) (b)

Dr. Derek Prince described as Holy Spirit anesthetic so there would be no pain or discomfort as they received spiritual surgery. The carpet becomes God's operating table.

(b) Judging by Manifestations.

Then again it is quite wrong to attempt to measure the amount of pollution in a person by their manifestations, that is, whether they manifest speedily or dramatically or not at all.

The usual error is to think that dramatic manifestations mean that a person is severly demonized and vice versa, but in point of fact **the more a sufferer has the Holy Spirit and lives close to the Lord, the more likely they are to manifest dramatically and quickly.** On the other hand a person locked up in depression or schizophrenia or very heavily bound in spiritual chains may only manifest slightly, if at all. Some of the most committed and "full-on" Christians I know have experienced some very lively deliverance releases — until the power of God quietened them.

This may seem strange to you but very simply, it is easier to get good results quickly with people who are full of the Holy Spirit. So the bottom line is that **dramatic releases often means that a Christian has plenty of Holy Spirit power in them assisting their deliverance.**

(vi) Demonization.

It needs to be stated at the very outset that the terms "demon POSSESSION" or "POSSESSED" are unfortunate translations and should be eliminated from Christian usage. Doctrines have been based on them which are entirely unfounded and it would not be overstating the truth to say that there are no such words in the original Greek New Testament scriptures.

The word translated "demon-possessed" literally means "under the influence of demons", or more briefly, "demonized". It is therefore a very broad word which could legitimately be used of Mary Magdalene when demonized by seven (Luke 8:2) or the man who had Legion (4,000 to 6,000). "Demon POSSESSED" paints an extreme picture and limits the application to within the human body. "Demonized" however, could refer to demons within the body or ATTENDANT demons causing levitational and psychic phenomena within a family's home, for example, but outside the human body. The Word of God clearly indicates that unclean spirits occupy geographical places, as well as living creatures (Zech. 13:2, Matt. 12:43, Rev. 18:2), therefore creatures AND PLACES can be demonized!

It would be not only hurtful but untrue to call a person mildly affected by demons "demon-possessed". That there is a matter of degree can be clearly seen from the normal but unfortunate translation "SEVERELY DEMON-POSSESSED" in Matt. 15:22. The "SEVERELY" qualifies the degree and the phrase should be translated "severely demonized". Obviously **the translation "possessed" infers total ownership and allows no room for measure or degree at all.**

Because of the narrowness of the phrase "demon-possessed" there has been an attempt by some teachers to distinguish between this and being **"oppressed"** or **"tormented"** by demons (Luke 6: 18, Acts 5: 16) or **"having"** them (Acts 8:7, Mark 7:25 – literal), but a comparison between Mark 7:25 (having an unclean spirit) and Matt. 15:22 ("possessed by a demon", demonized) indicates that they are interchangeable terms used in the context of the same gospel incident. Once the broad and real meaning of "demon-possessed" is understood there is no need for such distinctions. A person or place oppressed by or having demons IS demonized! The question is "HOW BADLY?" and whether the term "demon-possessed" is ever justified for non-Christians. **It must never be used for Christians!**

(a) Can a Christian be Demonized?

It must be obvious that a person who is possessed by (belongs to) Christ cannot be demon-possessed, but the question should really be, "Can a Christian be demonized?" I think that from what I have been saying you will realize the answer has to be "Yes". At least 90% of the ministry between 1973–1976 was to people who had made some serious committal to Jesus Christ several years beforehand and some 44% of the folk claimed to be Spirit-filled because they spoke in tongues. Since that period the percentage of tongue-speaking Christians who have received ministry has increased steadily to approximately 85% in 1982. They seem to be more able to perceive their problems and also keener to shed them.

Some Christians teach that **every** Christian is filled with the Spirit, the basis of this stance being taken on the flimsiest textual evidence imaginable, misinterpreting Ephesians 5:18 and Colossians 2:10. They say that if we are sealed with the Holy Spirit we are AUTOMATICALLY FILLED with the Spirit. If that is the case, why is being filled with the Spirit a special condition for the selection of the seven deacons from the brethren (Acts 6:3)? Stephen was chosen as a deacon, and the conditions that the Apostles laid down for the selection of seven men were that they should be of good repute, "full of the Spirit". Now, if everybody is filled with the Holy Spirit in the Church of God, then obviously that condition has to be thrown out because it applies to everybody; one is not sorting people out at all. But if you have to select from the midst of you seven men of good repute and full of the Holy Spirit, obviously the latter term distinguishes them from perhaps the newer Christians who are coming into an experience of the Holy Spirit.

So it is a distinguishing term, and therefore a Christian can be sealed with the Holy Spirit but not necessarily "filled" — and that certainly means Christians can still house unclean spirits in their souls. If you doubt me, there is a very strong verse to this effect which Paul wrote to the troublesome Corinthian church, chiding them. He says, "For if someone comes and preaches another Jesus than the one we preached or **if you receive a different spirit from the one you received**, or if you accept a different Gospel from the one you accepted, **you submit to it readily enough**" (2 Cor. 11:4). He was very put out with the Corinthians at this point because they were so gullible, they swallowed anything that came along their way. The Apostles had preached to them, and they had accepted Christ as Lord of their lives; a church had been pioneered in that corrupt city and now they were getting itinerant preachers passing through all the time, some of whom were bringing a different gospel. They accordingly were receiving a different spirit[1] and addressing them, he said, "If someone comes and preaches another Jesus than the one we preached, or if you receive **a different spirit** from the one you received from us (which was, of course, the Holy Spirit) and you accept a different gospel from the one you accepted, you submit to it readily enough". You will fall for anything. Honestly, haven't you got any discernment? Why can you not discern that which is in accord with the Gospel which I brought to you? Why will you swallow all this other nonsense?

I think the above is a fair paraphrase or explanation of the Apostle's meaning, and indeed is very relevant for today. People are converted; they are new in the Faith and somebody latches on to them from some particular sectarian viewpoint and leads them astray e.g. maybe someone from the Watchtower Society or Mormonism or something perhaps a little bit off the track of the Christian Gospel and therefore not inspired by the Holy Spirit but a **different (counterfeit) spirit**.

It is very easy to be led away from Christ as the center of your faith unless you are grounded in the Word of God and you know exactly what Apostolic Christianity is all about. So, **one can have**

---

1 Compare the opposite situation in which Caleb found himself (Numbers 14:24).

the Holy Spirit and one can collect other miscellaneous spirits on the way as well, which would then make us a candidate for deliverance!

(b) A New Creation

That is really the thrust of that particular biblical passage (2 Cor. 11:4). However, some people may refer to the old and new creation passage (2 Cor. 5:17) to suggest that conversion means automatic deliverance from demons. To be consistent one must then claim that we become **literally** perfect or righteous at conversion, rather than **accounted** righteous in Christ, which of course, is untenable. So if one is going to say, "Oh, I am a new creature; all things have become new and right now I am as straight and clean as can be — I can't have an unclean spirit; that is not possible": then I would reply that you ought to be perfect in that case, so please demonstrate your cleanliness without fail every day or otherwise explain why you are not perfect. This argument cannot be sustained for very long because it confuses justification by faith (that is, being RECKONED perfect) with literal perfection or completed sanctification (cf. Hebrews 10:14). That is to say, it confuses our LEGAL standing of being reckoned perfect on account of our being pardoned through the Cross of Christ, with our EXPERIENCE of gradual change from a polluted person into more and more Christ-likeness (2 Cor. 3:18).

If that confuses you, let me put it this way. It is no help to say that your lack of perfection in your daily behavior is due to sin, the spiritual disease of the human heart, because in doing so you defeat the argument that you have become a TOTALLY new creature because ALL THINGS have become new! *IF YOU CAN HAVE SIN IN YOUR HEART YOU CAN HAVE AN UNCLEAN SPIRIT ALSO.* Don't let anyone tell you that the notion of a mixture in the soul is a new doctrine. More than 200 years ago the famous and fiery American Calvinist Jonathon Edwards wrote:

"Lukewarmness in religion is abominable and zeal an excellent grace; yet above all other Christian virtues, it needs to be strictly watched and searched; for tis that with which corruption, and particularly pride and human passion is exceedingly apt to mix unobserved ... Yea the same persons may be the subject of much of the influences of the Spirit of God, and yet in some things be led away by the delusions of the devil, and this be no more of a paradox than many other things that are true of real saints, in the present state, where grace dwells with so much corruption, and the new man and the old man subsist together in the same person; and the Kingdom of God and the kingdom of the devil remain for a while together in the same heart."

We will have more to say about this under the heading "Beware the Counterfeit" in Chapter 3.

Becoming a new creation (2 Cor. 5:17) is obviously referring to a situation, a fresh start, the beginning of a new life in Christ and what has passed away is the lordship of satan and the reign (as kings) of sin, death and unclean spirits. One no longer has to accept their dominion ANY MORE. Praise the Name of the Lord!

(c) Light and Darkness.

Some teachers say that if a person has the Holy Spirit dwelling in them, then it is impossible to have an indwelling unclean spirit, because the Holy and the unclean cannot dwell together. This would mean, if it were a true description of a Christian's spiritual state, that a true Christian could never have an indwelling unclean spirit or be inwardly demonized.

The notion that a Christian cannot be demonized from within

is usually based on the scripture that light cannot dwell with darkness side by side. However when the Holy Spirit indwells us it is not for the purpose of dwelling peaceably side by side with darkness but to wage war — toe to toe. **Our conversion by the Spirit is the beginning, not the end, of the war in our souls**.

May I also point out that many of the scriptures pertaining to the subject of light and darkness seem to favor this view, while none can really be said to be in opposition:

> "... the light shines in the darkness and the darkness has not overcome (overtaken) it."
>
> John 1:5

> "... walk while you have the light, lest darkness overtakes you ..."
>
> John 12:35

> "I have come as light into the world, in order that all who believe in me may not remain in the darkness."
>
> John 12:46

> "... God is light and in Him is no darkness — none!"
>
> 1 John 1:5

> "... the darkness is passing away and the true light already shines. He who says he is in the light and hates his brother is still in the darkness. He who loves his brother continues in the light and there is no cause for stumbling with him."
>
> 1 John 2:8–10

The emphasis in all these scriptures seems to be:

(i)   the light of God is at war with the darkness of this world (cf. Eph.6:12, Phil. 2:15, Col. 1:13).

(ii) it is an ongoing battle AFTER CONVERSION for every Christian.

There is nothing in these verses to support the heresy that a soundly converted Christian cannot have a demon, but quite the opposite, seeing that the war against darkness we are all engaged in is a spiritual one (Eph. 6:12).

Until now, many Christians have been concerned about whether sins were caused by the activity or inspiration of the **root of sin** within the human heart or an **unclean spirit**. For example, a professing Christian steals from another man. Was it sin inspiring a theft or was it an unclean spirit of stealing?[1] This is an important question for every Christian who distinguishes between sin and unclean spirits because the **Christian solution** will vary accordingly. If a minister believes that the root of sin caused the action of stealing, he may not do much more than rebuke, counsel, pray, and hope it doesn't happen again. If he believes that a demon is responsible he will do all the above PLUS cast out the demon(s) in Jesus' Name.

The first ministry seeks to **CONTROL** the problem, the second ministry **REMOVES** the root cause of the problem and therefore advances Christian growth, the fullness of the Holy Spirit, and Christ-likeness much more rapidly.

Which ministry do you think is the perfect will of God for His people?

"But", you say, "If it is the root of sin causing the trouble, ministering deliverance could cause confusion, or even **psychological damage?**"

No — not at all. That theory can be discarded as a piece of intellectual, uninformed fear-mongering. It is empty sophistry[2]. Does not the Word of God say to test the spirits? (1 John 4:1). Plainly this encouragement is not only directed to the lying spirits that prophesy, in order to expose false prophets, but has the **widest possible application for the revealing of truth and**

---

1 This question assumes that SIN and unclean spirits are mutually exclusive. This matter will be discussed in Book 4.

2 In plain English — a load of meaningless rubbish.

error (1 John 4:6, cf. 1 Cor. 12:10, Heb. 5:14).

If a Christian believes that they may have an unclean spirit OR a minister believes that one of his flock may have an unclean spirit OR either simply wants to find out the truth, there is nothing wrong with them getting together for a session of deliverance ministry, and invoking the Holy Spirit to search out the believer's soul.

One cannot get rid of an unclean spirit if it is not there, any more than one can get blood out of a stone: and should such spiritual examination prove fruitful it is cause for joy not alarm. Whichever way the testing goes, both minister and sufferer should be delighted to discover the true situation.

Apparent **"psychological damage" should be seen for what it really is** — a batch of unclean spirits panicking because they have been uncovered and are in serious danger of getting evicted — to their own great disadvantage and to the glory of God!

None of these false notions stand up when measured against the Word of God. The great apostle Paul freely confessed that:

(i)   he continued to lose battles with the root of sin which dwelt with him (Rom. 7:14–20),

(ii) **nothing good dwells in his flesh** (Rom. 7:18),

(iii) his flesh and his spirit (the inner man) waged war continuously within him (Rom. 7:22–23).

So there we have it. We have it from the "Spirit-filled" apostle himself. Good and evil (Rom. 7:21–22) do not dwell harmoniously alongside each other within a man, but **they wage vigorous war within man**, the Holy and the human spirit against what is in the flesh, in the battleground of the soul.

The relationship between sin and unclean spirits will be explored in Book 4, but for now it is sufficient for us to establish the principle that if you can have sin in your heart you can have an unclean spirit also, and that "filled with the Spirit" apostles are no different from anyone else in this matter.

In later chapters it is made very plain that this ministry of **deliverance is basically for believers**, Christians who belong to Christ because they have received the seal of His Holy Spirit (Rom. 8:9b). If a person was totally delivered at conversion we certainly would not need the ministry at all. *IN NORMAL CIRCUMSTANCES* I would not dare to minister deliverance to a non-Christian because if they did not receive the Holy Spirit immediately afterwards, their unfortunate state could become seven times worse (Matt. 12:45). People who say that Christians cannot be demonized have very little use, if any, for the ministry at all.

Thus far we have said that a Christian can be demonized, that is, influenced by demons, and let us remember that the Lord Jesus subjected Himself to their fiery darts for our sakes, without sinning (which is more than we can say) but was not influenced by them, and that satan had **NOTHING in Him** (John 14:30). Therein is the difference!

(vii) Filled with the Spirit.

You may not have any difficulty in accepting that Christians who have RECEIVED the Holy Spirit may have unclean spirits in their souls also. BUT how do you feel about Christians who believe they have been FILLED with the Spirit? Surely it must be perfectly obvious from pastoral experience and observation that many who claim to be FILLED with the Holy Spirit have demonic problems also, but how can we reconcile this theologically? Personally I don't have any problem with this at all, but firstly we must resolve what we mean by the terms we use.

There are at least four (4) possible ways of understanding the term "filled with the Spirit", viz:

(1) The filling is **temporary** and given to meet special challenges confronting ministers of the early church.

This meaning is certainly true (Acts 4:8, 4:31, 6:8, 7:54–55, 13:9–10, 52). Do you know anyone that is filled with the Spirit ALL of the time? 80% of the time? 50% of the time? Maybe 10% of the time? !! Who is to say? How do we measure such things? No wonder Luke was so careful in the choosing of his words when recording the moving of the Spirit upon and in people's hearts! (Acts 8:15–18, 10: 44–45, 11:15, 19:6). I wish we were as careful today, instead of flinging the term "filled with the Spirit" around so loosely.

(2) The filling is really only in the nature of a "**topping up to overflowing**" without guaranteeing the complete removal of all rubbish.

This is also true. If one can view the soul pictorially in the shape of a glass or jar, half-full of dirt representing the sin and the agencies of satan, the biggest and heaviest dirt would normally be at the bottom of the glass[1] with smaller and lighter stones on top and covered again by small, loose stones and fine dust and dirt. Drowning in this muck is the human spirit "dead in trespasses and sin" until the Holy Spirit is invited in to rule over the whole mess and make alive the human spirit again. When the Holy Spirit flows in (like water) and fills the soul, much of the light-weight dirt will flow over the brim, and the soul may know a release from many unclean drives and emotions that were a part of the old nature.

However, no matter how much one is filled to overflowing and no matter how much of the light-weight dirt is carried away, the heavy stones remain at the bottom of the glass (soul). These will not normally go until authority is taken over them. The "strong" (man) of the house must be bound and the authority and power of the Lord Jesus Christ brought to bear against them by SPECIFIC

---

1 See diagram Book 3 Chap. 8 (iii) (b)

DELIVERANCE, perhaps with prayer and fasting, in order to remove rulers and authorities of satan.

(3) The filling is **permanent** and **complete** and thus no unclean spirit can remain or be present.

True of the Lord Jesus Christ but NOT of the people of God, at least until just before the Rapture. Jesus, of course, was FULLY filled with the Spirit at His baptism by John (Luke 4:1). Why is this true only of Jesus, and not of us? Simply because He was conceived and born without taint of sin, and satan had NO THING in Him (John 14:30) — no sin, no death, no unclean spirit. Therefore Jesus could be (and was) FULLY filled with the Holy Spirit! Hallelujah!

(4) A **combination** of (1) and (2).

It must be obvious that if both (1) and (2) are true for the people of God, then they are complementary and I believe that these two meanings together give us the understanding we are seeking. Therefore for the purposes of clarity I suggest that people who are TOPPED UP can be described as filled with the Spirit and those who have been totally cleansed of unclean spirits (know anyone?) can be described as FULLY filled with the Spirit.

Whatever YOU might understand the term to mean, the problem remains that the "spiritual territory" (i.e. the soul) of a Christian can be occupied by both the Holy Spirit and an unclean spirit and somewhere in the middle, taking sides(?), is the human spirit. The human spirit **should** be in full harmony and submission to the Holy Spirit because, after all, it invited the Spirit to come in, but alas! we know from experience, commitment and submission in theory can be quite different from commitment and submission in actual daily practice. It is important to clear up our understanding of these matters, because otherwise the danger remains that SOME Christians are going to refrain from the deliverance for which their soul is crying out, simply because they think they are FULLY filled with the Spirit. Their full salvation is affected by the error, and that is very serious!

The conclusions that flow from all that we have said in this section are that:

1. A Christian CANNOT be "demon-possessed".

2. A Christian CAN be demonized from within, as well as from without.

3. **Spirit-filled Christian CAN be demonized from within, as well as from without.**

4. A FULLY Spirit-filled Christian is not demonized from within but will experience attacks from without, like Jesus experienced in the wilderness.

2. The Widespread Need and Scope of the Ministry.

We all sense the bottomless pit of poor health, both physical and mental, around us and, with the exception of a few congregations upon which an active healing and deliverance ministry is exercised, the ailing health of the world is also the experience of Christians.

Newspapers regularly report that our worst fears are true. A survey in 1972 observed that **15% of the Australian population are constantly ill** — disabled in some way by chronic illness. The survey results were released by the **Medical Journal of Australia** and said that 116 in each 1000 suffered from rheumatism or arthritis or both, 79 from hay fever, 40 from asthma, 7 from diabetes and 14 from congenital illness. Chest pain and shortness of breath, indicating heart disease, were found to be symptoms with the greatest disabling potential. More than 12% of the population suffers nervous or personality disorders, or headaches, and it seems that suffering from "nerves" is no longer considered disgraceful, the survey said.

A Sydney physician, lecturing nurses in a large public hospital said **there is no scientific reason or cause for death**, and he is right. We may talk about this or that wearing out or breaking down, but the actual visitation of death itself is unexplainable. **Death is not an expectation of man** and we have to teach our children that everything living in the physical world must die one day, because it is not "naturally inherent" in man to expect to die or to have a temporary existence. We have to be taught this by life's experiences with pets and animals and the older members of our families.

The scriptures tell us that **sin and death** entered the human race through Adam and spread to all men and we see the truth of this all around us. As men and women get older the sin begins to show on their faces and as the spirit of death manifests himself more and more, the outward flesh becomes more and more corrupted, until some of us, if there is no scientific explanation for our death, are said to die from old age, or degenerative disease. We just wear out, they say; but why?

What is degenerative disease? Simply the deposit of death within us over-ruling our bodily systems with decay. Thanks be to God we Christians are no longer under the dominion of death but have eternal life in Christ Jesus, with indestructible, imperishable, glorious spiritual bodies awaiting us. Hallelujah! O death, where is thy sting, O grave, where is thy victory?

Mental Health. The situation with mental illness is rapidly becoming frightening. As more and more people experience mental sickness, facilities available for treatment become exhausted and the sufferer is thrust back into the world and endeavours to learn to cope. **Dr. Cominos**, Senior Psychologist at Walston Park Mental Hospital is quoted as saying that **four out of ten** Australians (a people of sunshine, beaches and easy-going life-style) are suffering from mental ill-health to some degree. Dr. Cominos stressed that the community should become more aware of the **tremendous numbers of people IN THEIR MIDST who require mental treatment** (Telegraph 1/11/71). It is much worse today in 1991!

Another survey conducted by **Dr. A.J. McMichael** and **Professor B.S. Hetzel** of the Department of Social and Preventative Medicine at Monash University and published in the Medical Journal of Australia, reports that **nearly half** of the students at Melbourne University believed they were mentally ill — 49% reporting what they called "self-assessed mental illness" in their second year (Telegraph 25/4/75).

It is very difficult, says **Dr. W. Barclay**, Director of N.S.W. Psychiatric Services, to make an assessment of the actual figures of mentally ill people in Australia — one reason being that not all of them are in hospital. But there are roughly 9,500 in N.S.W. alone. Although most patients are discharged within six months of being admitted, the chances of illness recurring are high (Telegraph 25/8/71).

The upshot of all this psychiatric evidence is that the Christian will readily see that man's problems of physical and mental health are basically SPIRITUAL.[1] We cannot avoid the scriptural truth that **we do not contend with blood and flesh but with rulers and authorities** and spiritual hosts of wickedness in the heavenlies. We need to know that satan has a kingdom, that he has his kingdom on earth inasmuch as the whole world lies in the power of the evil one and it is this against which the Church is prevailing. The gates of Hades are the gates of the kingdom of satan but the question arises as to WHERE is this kingdom? If we look at the Kingdom of God we normally understand kingdom to mean "rule", and the scriptures indicate that when the Holy Spirit casts out demons, the rule or kingdom of satan is replaced by the Rule or Kingdom of God (Matt. 12:26–28). **The rule or kingdom of satan therefore resides in every heart where Christ**

1 Refer to our book "Mental Illness - What Can Christians Do?"

is not Lord. Such a kingdom reveals itself by the works of the flesh as against the fruit of the Spirit (Gal. 5:19–24) or by even more obvious demonic behavior.

It is obvious from this that the kingdom of satan on earth (which can be broken down into individual kingdoms in every unbelieving heart) is very large indeed NUMERICALLY speaking, but we need have no fear; there are more FOR us than against us (2 Kings 6:16).

It will not surprise you then when I say that the widespread prevalence of demonization, or shall I say, the potential of the ministry of deliverance, is extremely great, in my opinion. Perhaps the word "mammoth" would not be an exaggeration. Why? The view of those ministering deliverance is that compulsive alcoholics, for example, are enslaved by demons inspiring their bondage from within. If this is true, given 5 million inhabitants of Sydney and, for the purposes of this hypothesis, say 1 in 10 has a drink problem caused by a very conservative estimate of 10 demons of **alcohol** addiction, this produces a figure of 5 million demons of alcoholism within Sydneyites alone. The same for **homosexuals** — 5 million demons of sodomy within Sydneyites alone. This is not taking into consideration the spirits, unclean spirits or demons (these terms are used interchangeably throughout) still discarnate, and endeavoring to enter into living creatures (Matt. 12:43–45, Mark 5:1–20). We can only very roughly estimate ("guess" would be a better word) those indwelling humans. Add demons of **fear, terror** and **tension** (probably the most common form of demonic attack) plus the full range of **sexual** and **occult** spirits and one may be forced to the conclusion that every society on earth, both west and east, developed and underdeveloped, is not only surrounded by the principalities and powers of darkness but is riddled by them from within (Eph. 6:12). Satan is indeed the god and ruler of this world (2 Cor. 4:4. John 12:31) and the whole world does indeed lie in the power of the evil one (1 John 5:19). How much the world needed a saviour, and needs THE Saviour now!

Professor C.S. Lewis is often quoted as saying, "There are two equal and opposite errors into which our race can fall about devils (demons), one is to disbelieve in their existence and the other is to believe and feel an excessive and unhealthy interest in them". We need to remember that this was expressed when people may not have talked about demons very much at all, and I think he had great perception and spiritual insight into the scriptures to be able to say that when he said it. To quote him today may be valid, but we need to compare it with the Apostle Paul's inspired teaching that "**We are not contending against flesh and blood, but against the principalities, against the powers, against the world rulers of this present darkness, against the spiritual hosts of wickedness in the heavenly places**" (Eph. 6:12). He didn't say the Christian RARELY, or even SOMETIMES wrestles with principalities and powers of darkness. If language can be taken at its plain meaning and Paul's proposition is true, he is saying that **the enemies of the Christian are not physical but spiritual in EVERY avenue of life** (cf. 2 Cor. 10:3–4). This is not to be "demon-happy" but intensely practical by facing the truth. In other words, everything with which the Christian wrestles has a spiritual source that is hostile and antichrist. Now Paul said it — I didn't say it, except to quote him. If you want to say that Paul is demon-happy, that is your prerogative. That is what he wrote, being inspired by the Holy Spirit. So, accepting his word, we face a tremendous power of darkness and a widespread, powerful authority against us. And I think when we realise that, then we begin to realise what the **victory of the Cross**[1] really means. It gives us an even greater understanding of the overwhelming nature of the victory of the shed Blood of Calvary that rendered all this power, all these principalities, the world rulers of this present darkness, as something to be trodden under our feet. The more we look at the Scripture, the more the wonder of the Cross is enlarged and magnified, and to "put down" deliverance

1 See next chapter

is to impinge on the victory of the Cross; Jesus' victory becomes smaller because we are told the enemy is not so big, important or widespread. He is only a little ruler with a little kingdom that might occasionally come to attack us and in the West, of course, we don't have to worry about that. It is only the primitive, disease-ridden, poor people of the world who need the missionaries, and perhaps deliverance (they say). **You know that is not true, and I know it's not true.** So Professor Lewis was very helpful in his time and I think it is still possible to be demon-happy. We wouldn't want to make the mistake of thinking and talking about them all the time. We must remember the victory and when we have to think of the enemy, it is only to give us an awareness of what we are up against. That also gives us an awareness of the previous victory which has been purchased for us, and so Professor Lewis' caution is perhaps still valid in many ways.

But if anybody said to me, "Oh! Peter, you are demon-happy", I would say to them, "Well, most evangelical Christians are considered sin-happy; everything is sin; sin is preached continuously to the lost world. We are always talking about sin. Why are we always talking about sin? Because it is a very real disease; it is a very real enemy; and **one has to expose the problem before one can provide the solution.** Well, when we talk about demons we are only talking about the things that have a big part to play in sin[1] — so if it's right for me to emphasize sin, then it's also right for me to expose demons". But it all leads to the solution, who is Jesus.

The tendency of the world, and at the present point in time, of the Church also, is to downgrade the ministry and minimize it as much as possible. This is based on the premise that cases of demonization are quite rare, and satan would certainly like us all to believe this. But perhaps the most subtle put-down of all is the notion that Christians should not dwell in their thoughts

---

1 See "End-Time Deliverance" or Book 4 "We All Have Our Demons."

upon the person of satan and his followers. We are encouraged to look at Jesus and the victory, and forget the powers of darkness. Attractive as this may sound, it contains only a part of the truth.

If we truly keep our spiritual eyes on Jesus, He will reveal to us from His Word the nature, strengths and weaknesses of the enemy we are to engage in battle. "Looking unto Jesus" does not mean becoming a spiritual ostrich and hiding our heads in the sand, pretending satan doesn't exist or just ignoring him and hoping that he will retreat from us because we are "in Christ". The scripture says, **"Resist the devil and he will flee from you — draw near to God and He will draw near to you"**, so it is not an "either-or" situation but a "both-and" situation. It is not "resist the devil OR draw near to God". It is not "Look to Jesus for victory OR examine the powers of darkness closely" but it is "Look to Jesus for victory AND examine them" — not for the purpose of glorifying them or being contaminated by them, but that we might put our feet on their necks as was illustrated for us in the story of Joshua and the five evil, occult kings:

> **"And when they brought those kings out to Joshua, Joshua summoned all the men of Israel, and said to the chiefs of the men of war who had gone with him, 'Come near, put your feet upon the necks of these kings.' Then they came near, and put their feet upon the necks and Joshua said to them, 'Do not be afraid or dismayed; be strong and of good courage; for thus the Lord will do to all your enemies against whom you fight.'"**
> Joshua 10:24–25

Just as Joshua made his captains ACT OUT their victory, if we are truly looking to Jesus, He will teach us spiritual warfare and use us to great effect in obtaining the victory we want to see.

One word of warning. We don't need to sample satan to know him. We don't need to experience seances or read occult books or risk contaminating ourselves to know the enemy. **All we need**

to know is in the Bible. The Word of God is indeed sufficient (2 Tim. 3:16–17) and our knowledge should only come from or be in harmony with that Word. Obviously **battle experience will enable us to understand that Word more clearly as the Holy Spirit teaches us.**

The ministry of deliverance helps us to understand even more of the overwhelming nature of the victory of the shed Blood of Calvary that rendered all the ugly powers and principalities, the world rulers of this present darkness, as of no account, to be trodden under our feet. The victory of the Cross is enlarged and magnified because there the Lord Jesus made the powers of darkness an open spectacle and put them to shame. **To minimize demonology is to minimize the Victory.** If we say that demonization is rare in the West except for mental cases, and it is only the primitive people on the mission fields who need deliverance, we:

(i) **deceive ourselves**

(ii) **unwittingly denigrate Christ's redeeming work on the Cross**

(iii) **are tragically inhibited in our diagnosis of the spiritual needs around us.**

If we take Paul's words (Eph. 6:12, 2 Cor. 10:3–4) as literal statements of truth, it becomes very difficult to sustain the view that cases of demonization are rare; rather the evidence supports the view that FREEDOM from demonization is rare.

It is this very concept which has created opposition to the deliverance ministry. There is, I believe, an enormous reluctance to face the mind-boggling consequences of this revelation, as it reaches into every Christian family. Look at it this way — few Christians will deny the reality and activity of sin and the flesh in their lives; for the moment all I am asking you to consider is the extent of the relationship between sin, the flesh, the devil and the powers of darkness — and remember that deliverance very often helps when all other forms of Christian aid have fallen short. I have often been asked on what scriptural authority do I base my view that human personality difficulties such as fear, resentment, guilt, terror, depression, frustration, anger, murder, destruction, lying, deceit, sorrow etc. etc., may be caused by the activity of unclean spirits, when the scriptures do not give detailed information. The answer is that once the spiritual warfare between Christ and satan is clearly defined, there are enough examples, such as lying spirits causing prophets to lie (1 Kings 22:19–23)[1] and Legion, to establish links between immoral, ugly or destructive human behavior and demons. The scriptures only require the evidence of two or three testimonies to establish a matter and therefore do not give us a detailed list of antichrist's activities simply because the list would be endless (as endless and as boring as a telephone book!), while the outward forms of attack, especially those of an occult character (e.g. eastern mysticism) may change from age to age. It is sufficient for the Word of God to give us the principles, to be applied by discerning Christian soldiers in the age in which they live.

In my view it should not be too much to ask of a Christian that when he repents daily for his sins, he recognizes where demons have led him astray; as it can be demonstrated from the Scriptures that demons cause sin, false worship and false teaching amongst other things.[2] Therefore it is not horrible, disgraceful or insulting for a Pastor to say that someone is being spiritually attacked or affected by demons. He is simply telling a Bible truth that applies

---

1 e.g. the spirit of ...

jealousy	Num.5:14	stupor	Romans 11:8
pride	Eccles. 7:8	fear	2 Tim. 1:7
whoredom	Hosea 4:12, 5:4	antichrist	1 John 4:3
python	Acts 16:16	error	1 John 4:6
bondage to fear	Romans 8:15	infirmity	Luke 13:11

2 Appendix D. Bible Notes on Demonology.

to everyone[1] — and facing the truth without fuss is essential if the enemy is to be put to flight.

3. THE OCCULT AREA

(i) Old Testament Warnings

> "When you come into the land which the LORD your God gives you, you shall not learn to follow the abominable practices of those nations. There shall not be found among you anyone who burns his son or his daughter as an offering, anyone who practices divination, a soothsayer, or an augur, or a sorcerer, or a charmer, or a medium, or a wizard, or a necromancer. **For whoever does these things is an abomination to the LORD**; and because of these abominable practices the LORD your God is driving them out before you. You shall be blameless before the LORD your God. For these nations, which you are about to dispossess, give heed to soothsayers and to diviners; but as for you, the LORD your God has not allowed you to do so".
>
> Deuteronomy 18:9–14

The passage above contains in the broadest terms most of the areas of the occult with which the Church is grappling today. **Divination** could cover today either water divination or mineral divination etc., and not excluding clairvoyance or any area whereby the gift of the Holy Spirit known as "the word of knowledge" (1 Cor. 12:8) is counterfeited, for divination is taken to mean knowledge divined by non-Christian power and/or

---

1 For further expansion of this point, please refer to Book 4 "We All Have Our Demons" or "End-Time Deliverance."

non-natural power. **Soothsaying** appears to be the equivalent of modern foretelling or fortune telling. An **augur** is one who divines or gains knowledge by omens; a **sorcerer** (literally "**druggist**" but usually translated "witchcraft") to be one who dabbles with drugs or witchcraft or both; **a charmer to be one who is able to induce trances or obtain power or control over the actions and responses of another through spells or hypnosis**; a medium to be one who is a consulter with familiar spirits, or a spiritualist, or one who makes any attempt to contact the dead; a **wizard** to be one who dabbles in the practice of magic; a **necromancer** to be one who endeavors to predict the future or gain information by means of the dead.

All these broad definitions are perhaps brief and inadequate, but it is difficult to find anything more accurate and concise, and of course, they tend to overlap considerably.

(ii) Spiritualism (Spiritism).

Experience so far in the field of actual ministry to occult-oppressed subjects strongly indicates that the biblical warnings of the Old Testament given through Moses are one hundred percent valid for today, and evidence that the principalities and powers of darkness (Eph. 2:2, 6:12) are indeed responsible for these activities is found in the New Testament. Although there are obviously frauds in the psychic business, the reality of genuine spiritualism may be supported from the scriptures (medium of Endor: 1 Sam. 28:8–19), but it is important to note that the scriptures only admit the possibility of contacting the dead when the dead are in **Paradise**; that is to say, the dead are those who have "died in the Lord". The witch or medium of Endor raised up an appearance of the dead prophet **Samuel at the request of King Saul, but the story clearly indicates that Samuel was most unhappy at being disturbed and pronounced a curse upon Saul and his household**, to take effect the next day, i.e. the wiping out, by death, of his household and name in Israel forever. The fact remains that **attempts to contact the dead, whether they be in Paradise or in Hades, are an abomination to the Lord and are totally forbidden**.

Further, the scriptures indicate that it is impossible for the dead who are suffering in Hades to appear to their families who are still alive on earth. In the story of the beggar Lazarus who went to Paradise (Abraham's bosom) and the rich man who went to Hades, it is plain that it is impossible to change from Hades to Paradise or from Paradise to Hades. But the main point for us is that the rich man in Hades **cannot** appear to his living relatives to warn them personally of the dire results of living a fleshly, extravagant and ungodly life; and the second point is that the rich man appeals to Abraham to send someone from Paradise, so apparently this is a possibility — but the request is rejected on the grounds that the rich man's family have Moses (the Law) and the Prophets, i.e. **the Word of God**, to guide them through this life into the next, if they will accept it (Luke 16:19–31).

So it must be asked, if contacting the dead can only be successfully achieved with those in Paradise, even though this be a flagrant act of rebellion against God's Word, how do spirits and mediums make contact with the departed dead so freely and regularly? — especially as many have died without any evidence of following the Christian faith?

The answer is simply that spiritists and mediums do NOT contact the dead, i.e. departed **human** spirits at all. They make contact with **familiar** spirits, i.e. demons which have sufficient knowledge of the intimate details of the deceased's life as to be able to pass themselves off as a departed human spirit. The Bible calls them "familiar spirits" because they are indeed familiar with intimate family details — they may even have resided in the soul of the deceased while they were alive, in their role as an unclean spirit.

In summary, the Bible affirms that **it is not possible to contact the dead in Hades,** i.e. those who have died outside of the Christian faith, and also that ANY attempt to contact the dead, either in Paradise or Hades is SPIRITISM — a form of witchcraft — and brings the anger of God upon its perpetrators. Spiritism is a fraud carried out by the powers of darkness masquerading as the human spirits of departed love ones, and which manifest themselves through the avenue of earthly mediums, who are themselves deceived.

The bottom line is that **contacting the dead departed saints is sin, and is a characteristic of spiritism, not Christianity.**

Those trying to get help from St. Mary, St. Francis, St. Christopher or any other of the dead departed saints of God are making the same abominable error that King Saul made when he sought help from the dead departed prophet Samuel. This puts the Christian under the curse of spiritism, which curse should be broken[1] immediately by REPENTING and RENOUNCING the practice of contacting the departed saints (or anyone else, for that matter) in the NAME OF JESUS OF NAZARETH who took all our curses upon Himself (Gal. 3:10–14). Praise His Holy Name.

To discourage anyone procrastinating in this matter let me remind you that spiritism is in the realm of WITCHCRAFT, that MEDIUMS are the same (in the Word of God) as WITCHES or WITCHDOCTORS, and that experienced Deliverance Ministers[2] in three nations nominate the unclean spirit behind spiritism in the Churches as being the spirit of the arch-witch herself "Queen" JEZEBEL (Rev. 2:20–23, cf. Isa. 47:8–15, Rev. 17:1–7, 18:1–9).

---

1 An example of renouncing prayer can be found in Appendix E

2 Bill Subritzky (N.Z.) in "Demons Defeated" p. 26f. Gary and Ruth Penhall (Aust.), Mahesh Chavda (U.S.A.) and probably many others.

(iii) New Testament Evidence.

How can we make the mental jump from warnings regarding occult practices in the Old Testament to the conclusion that such practices are inspired by unclean spirits? Simply because that is exactly what the New Testament does, and not only regarding occult matters.

Although the New Testament speaks in many places about casting out demons, specific details are few and far between.

The incidents that are described more carefully therefore become KEY PASSAGES TO UNLOCK OUR UNDERSTANDING of the more general information. The Holy Spirit has provided evidence that the following specific areas have been the activity of unclean spirits:

1. **Osteogenic Bone afflictions**. The "daughter of Abraham" with the curvature of the spine is described as being bound by satan and having a spirit of infirmity. Once it is conceded that satan is responsible for a sickness, it would seem to be intellectually indefensible to deny the activity of an unclean spirit (Luke 13:10–16).

2. **Physical afflictions.** The dumb and deaf lad (Mark 9:25). The blind and dumb demoniac (Matt. 12: 22–24). These are PHYSICAL afflictions caused by spirits affecting the SENSE ORGANS.

3. **Mental disturbance.** Legion is generally considered the most extreme case in the scriptures and we know from a synopsis of the New Testament evidence that he was violent and suicidal, motivated by powerful and destructive forces. Psychotic, perhaps even homicidal, he was beyond human help and only the ministry of Christ could free him (Mark 5:1–20).

4. **Debilitating Mind Disorder.** The dumb and deaf lad (above) was apparently also epileptic (Matt. 17:15–18, Luke 9:39).

5. **Occult bondage.** The slave girl with a spirit of divination (a python) is the key incident. Notice that the occult inspiration speaks the truth but is apparently irritating and hindering the proclamation of God's Word. There is no request for help from the girl but the incident reveals a sharp conflict between the unclean spirit and the Holy Spirit. The unclean is no match (Acts 16:16–18).

There are some folk who believe one can be an occultist AND a Christian, many people wearing both Zodiac and other occult emblems around their necks together with Christian symbols such as a cross. If one is still unconvinced of the incompatibility of the two, there are a number of key texts in the New Testament where conflicts between the apostles and occult representatives or powers arises and which end in the routing of the forces of darkness, viz:

(1) **The magician Simon and the Apostle Peter** (Acts 8: 9–24). This is a classic case of **occult power** (v.9) **being attributed erroneously to God** (v.10) by the uninformed masses. **Not everything spiritual is of God!**

(2) **The magician Elymas and the Apostle Paul** (Acts 13: 7–12). The sharp clash between Elymas (v.8) and the Apostle is quite unlike the problem of the "sympathetic" Simon (above). The Apostle has no hesitation in applying his authority and power against the enemy for total victory in this revealing and **unusual miracle** incident.

(3) **Occult Practices and Magic Arts (curious things)** at Ephesus (Acts 19: 1–20). This experience of burning up expensive occult items and books (v.19) is being repeated today in every third world country where Christ is preached, while the "educated West" betrays its Christian heritage for a mess of occult pottage (cf. Deut. 7:25–26, 2 Kings 23:4f, 1 Chr. 14:12, 2 Chr. 15:16).

(4) **The stoicheia** are the spiritual elements of the universe (2 Peter 3:10, 12), i.e. demons or spirits of nature (Col. 2: 8, 20;

Gal. 4:8–9), and to return to them is considered apostasy by the Apostle Paul. We will say more about the stoicheia under the heading "**Creation spirits**".[1]

No New Testament study on the occult would be complete without taking into consideration the above references in their context, bearing in mind that, with experience, the gift of **discerning of spirits** (1 Cor. 12:10) is often evidenced in such confrontations.

The **Rev. Harold Dewberry**, one-time Director of **Teen Challenge** in Sydney and a Pastor with enormous deliverance experience by present-day standards, wrote in the February, 1974, issue of Teen Challenge:

> "The news media has been giving increased attention to the occult in recent weeks, particularly where school children are involved.
>
> On one occasion in a private high school all of a form of over 90 students admitted some involvement. Little is understood of the emotional repercussions of involvement and many suffer from 'psychic' weaknesses although there has been no personal involvement.
>
> This is one of the sins that is visited upon the children even up to the fourth generation.
>
> Fear, confusion, anxiety, depression and contention, with related hypertension, headaches, are the main emotional repercussions.
>
> Because involvement in the occult is breaking a command of God, repentance and confession is the way of (beginning) release."

1 Chap. 3,7 (i)

"Practices which can bring occult bondage include:
- having your fortune told by use of cards, tea leaves, palm reading etc.
- reading or following horoscopes.
- being hypnotised, practising self-hypnosis or yoga.
- attending a seance or spiritualist meeting.
- having a "life" or reincarnation meeting.
- consulting a ouija-board, planchette, cards or crystal ball.
- playing with so-called "games" of an occult nature such as ESP, telepathy, Kabala, etc.
- consulting a medium.
- seeking healing through magic conjuration and charming, through a spiritualist, Christian Scientist or anyone who practises "spirit-healing".
- seeking to consult missing persons or objects by consulting someone who has psychic powers.
- practising table-lifting, levitation or automatic writing.
- practising water divination.
- reading or possessing occult or spiritualist literature.
- **possessing occult or pagan objects.**
- having your handwriting analysed, practising mental suggestion, casting a magic spell or seeking psychic experiences"

Remember a basic principle of the Word of God "... at the mouth of two witnesses or at the mouth of three witnesses shall a matter be established" (Deut. 19:15). The Word of God has testified that human suffering in FIVE areas is caused by unclean spirits or demons, one area of which is the occult, not to mention the short list of sample spirits in the earlier footnote with the scripture references, and other areas of demonic activity noted in Appendix D under "Works of demons". If you still remain unconvinced, then there is nothing more I would want to say. You either believe the Word of God or you don't.

2

THE CHRISTIAN SOLUTION

INTRODUCTION

(i) The Cross

For the Christian, every solution to human need flows from the Cross of Calvary! Now that we have discussed the problems of the demonization of a human being, we must now consider the possible solutions, and draw attention to the BEST solution(s). But first, let me repeat again, that it is only through the Victory of the Cross of Jesus Christ by which we can get victory today over the powers of darkness. When the Lord was crucified as the Lamb of God who takes away the sin(s) of the World He LEGALLY established the defeat of the enemies of mankind. So much so that many Bible students confess that, although they have appreciated and received many benefits from their understanding of the Cross, the victory was so great that they still have not plumbed the depths of it all, and appropriated all that is available to them from that Sacrifice.

To put this victory into even sharper focus for us today, I offer for your consideration the following LEGAL victories obtained for us by Jesus Christ, with those victories that obviously relate to Deliverance and Healing in bold type:

ON THE CROSS THE LORD JESUS CHRIST LEGALLY DEALT WITH:

1. THE WORLD

"... glory in the Cross of our Lord Jesus Christ through which the WORLD has been crucified to me, and I to the WORLD."

Gal. 6:14

2. OUR FLESH

"God sent His own Son ... and condemned SIN in the FLESH."

Rom. 8:3

3. OUR WEAKNESSES AND DISEASES

"He took our weaknesses and bore our diseases."

Matt. 8:17

4. OUR SORROWS, PAINS, GRIEFS AND SICKNESSES

"He was despised and rejected (forsaken) of men, a man of SORROWS (PAINS) and **acquainted with GRIEF (SICKNESS)** and as one from whom men hide their face he was despised and we esteemed him not.

Surely (certainly, for sure) he has borne our GRIEFS (SICKNESSES) and carried our SORROWS (PAINS): yet we did esteem Him stricken, smitten of God and afflicted.

Yet it pleased the LORD to BRUISE him; he has put him to GRIEF (MADE HIM SICK) ..."

Isaiah 53:3–4, 10

5. Our Rejection and Loneliness

"He was DESPISED and REJECTED of men ... and as one from whom men hide their face. He was DESPISED and we did NOT ESTEEM Him."

Isa. 53:3, cf. Ps. 22:1 with Matt. 27:46, Matt. 8:20, Mark 10:29–31

6. Our Sins, Transgressions and Iniquities

"But he was wounded for our TRANSGRESSIONS, he was BRUISED for our INIQUITIES: the chastisement of our peace was upon him; and **by his stripes** (lit. **BRUISE** — singular) **WE ARE HEALED.**"

Isa. 53:5, cf. Rom. 5:8, 1 John 3:8, See Gen. 3:15 and 1 Peter 2:24 re: BRUISE

7. Our Heart Root Disease of Sin

"Behold, the Lamb of God who takes away the SIN of the World."

John 1 :29, cf. Rom. 6:6–7, 2 Cor. 5:21, 1 John 1:7–8

8. Spiritual Rulers and Authorities

God ... **"has taken it (the Old Covenant of justice and death) out of the way, nailing it to the Cross; putting off the RULERS and AUTHORITIES (of darkness). He (God) made them an open spectacle, triumphing over them in Him (Jesus)."**

Col. 2:14a–15

9. The Elemental Spirits

"If you died with Christ to the ELEMENTAL SPIRITS of the World, why do you live in the World as if subject to them?"

Col. 2:20, cf. v. 8, also Gal. 4:8–11

10. OUR OLD MAN (NATURE)

"We know that our OLD MAN was crucified with (Christ), that the body of sin might be destroyed, that we should no longer be enslaved by sin."

Rom. 6:6

11. THE CURSE OF THE LAW

Christ redeemed us out of the CURSE OF THE LAW, becoming a curse on our behalf, for it is written, "All are accursed who hang on a tree."

Gal. 3:13, cf. Deut. 21:22–23, Col. 2:15

12. THE CURSE OF CREATION (THORNS)

" ... CURSED IS THE GROUND for your sake. In toil shall you eat of it all the days of your life. THORNS AND THISTLES shall it bring forth to you ... In the sweat of your face shall you eat bread ..."

Gen. 3:17–19, cf. Heb. 6:8, John 19:1–6

13. DEATH

"Death is swallowed up in victory. O death, where is thy victory? O death, where is thy sting? The sting of DEATH is sin, and the power of sin is the law. But thanks be to God, who gives us the victory through our Lord Jesus Christ."

1 Cor. 15:54–57, cf. Ps. 23:4,
Rom. 6:8–11, Heb. 2:14–15

14. THE WORKS OF THE DEVIL

"The reason the Son of God was manifested was to LOOSE (DESTROY) THE WORKS OF THE DEVIL."

1 John 3:8

"...God anointed Jesus of Nazareth with the Holy Spirit and Power, who went about doing good and **CURING ALL THOSE WHO WERE OPPRESSED BY THE DEVIL**, because God was with him."

Acts 10:38

Please notice that I have only put those texts in bold print which OBVIOUSLY relate to unclean spirits, deliverance and healing!

Dr. Leon Morris, a conservative Bible scholar of world repute, has written:

> We do not always realise that the Cross is concerned with our body. Matthew quotes Isaiah 53:4 with respect to the healing activities of Jesus: "He himself took our weaknesses and bore our sicknesses" (Matthew 8:17).
>
> Now that passage from Isaiah is one of the classic passages for the atonement, bringing out the truth that Christ bore our sins. What Matthew is telling us is that in bearing our sins Christ also did something about this perennial problem of our sickness.

(ON BEING Magazine – March 1989)

It would be wrong to imply that Dr. Morris agrees with us without qualification, but the above is a significant beginning. He goes on to say: "**In all this (consideration of the Cross) we discover that the atonement is vaster and deeper than any of the traditional theories affirms.**"

Amen! Now let us consider the application of the Victory of the Cross by means of the various ministries available to demonised sufferers.

It bears repeating from time to time that Deliverance is a love ministry. I suppose one could say that about every genuine ministry of Christ, but I say it here because I deem it virtually impossible to **maintain a regular deliverance ministry** without being constrained by the love of Christ for the sea of suffering humanity around us which is being devoured by spiritual wolves.

One can even preach and teach for selfish motives over the long term (Phil. 1:15–18) and only the Lord knows about it, but I don't think that it is possible with deliverance. After a few years in this ministry many leaders look for an easier way of service, even a way out altogether, and I have been no exception. Praise God He has shown me an easier way, which we will reveal in Book 2 "Engaging the Enemy", but we must first lay our foundations here, upon which we can build for a lasting and effective ministry.

(ii) The Power of Love

Father Lazarus Moore of the **Russian Orthodox Church (Abroad)** told me how he once was led by the Holy Spirit to visit a recluse, a hermit living in the Ukrainian mountains. The man was reputed to be mad, but Lazarus obediently set out up a mountain-side where the hermit was reported to live. As he clambered up, a man came flying out of a cave some 50 metres ahead and came charging down the mountain side, his arms flailing, his face contorted, and making weird and frightening noises. As the distance closed between them Lazarus didn't know what to do, but he stood his ground and sent up a "flash prayer" of desperation (Acts 2:21). The man reached Lazarus and grasped him in a fierce bear-hug, so Lazarus hugged him back — **with the love of Christ**.

Within seconds the pair of them were weeping on each other's shoulder as all the violence and destruction began to leave the man. It seems they continued until the man was restored into his right mind. Such can be the power of love that flows from faith, obedience and faith again.

(iii) The Power of the Word of God

The Bible Society in Australia reported an interesting story in its June 1989 edition of "**The Sower:**"

> Dianne is employed by the Aboriginal Congress of the Uniting Church and is doing translation work in the Djambarrpuynu language at Elcho Island off the coast of Arnhem Land in the Northern Territory.
>
> Her story of the emotional reaction to the reading of the Scriptures began when a young man who had never made any sort of Christian commitment but was well thought-of on the Island had expressed an interest in checking the Djambarrpuynu Bible translation.
>
> "So I asked for his help and he was really keen.
>
> "I took a few spare copies of the manuscript (Luke) and passed them around, and we read slowly, sentence by sentence, so that we could discuss it. From the beginning he was really excited about it ... and affected others with his excitement.
>
> "We were well into the first chapter one day when **he gave a really violent shiver and then came out in the goose bumps on his legs** and said, "Look what that did to me!"
>
> "It happened a number of times thereafter."

This account underlines two things for us, that (i) the Word of God can and does operate the power of God in sovereign ways at times, and (ii) **mature Christians are often unable to interpret the symptoms of a Deliverance Cycle.**[1] This story would have

---

1 Book 3 *Walking in Victory* Chap.7, 1.

passed through many editorial hands before publication but, on the face of it, no one (from beginning to end) seems to have understood its real significance. Amazing.

Perhaps we should add here that **prayer and fasting** are often engaged in for deliverance and we will say more about this under the heading of "Healing."

(iv) The Power of Conversion

In some cases today **Christian conversion** appears to have been effective in healing past associations and practices of an occult character, but it has to be added that there are very many Christians for whom normal conversion and spiritual growth through **sanctification** has not had the desired effect of removing occult principalities and powers. **It is incontestable that mature Christians may suffer from a whole range of psychiatric disorders**, and psychiatrists appear to have a growing awareness of the evidence of occult practices as a primary cause of mental disturbance. This has certainly been the case with troubled Christians seeking the ministry of deliverance from Christian ministers, a significant number of whom had already received professional psychiatric attention.

For the mental and physical infirmities or weaknesses of men, the Bible presents at least three possible supernatural solutions through the ministry of our Lord Jesus Christ i.e. **preaching the gospel, healing the sick** and **casting out demons**. There are good reasons to believe that the latter terms are not exclusive but rather mutually inclusive in confirmation of the preached Word, although healing and casting out demons (deliverance) may be distinguished from each other in that healing is normally related to the flesh (physical body) and deliverance is a ministry directed to the unclean spirits — which may be the root-cause of sickness in the flesh. Broadly speaking, people are **healed in the flesh from physical problems**, and **delivered in the soul from spiritual**

problems, and it is all done by the supernatural ministry of the Holy Spirit; but we need to remember that even when we engage physical problems **we do not wrestle with blood and flesh but with (spiritual) rulers and authorities etc.** The order of words "blood and flesh" (rather than our modern "flesh and blood") recorded in the original Greek scriptures simply underlines the primacy of blood in spiritual warfare, because:

(i) **the (human) spirit is in the soul** (Gen. 2:7, Heb. 4:12, Luke 1:46–47),

(ii) **the soul is in the blood** (Levit. 17:11, 14, Deut. 12:23) and

(iii) the blood is in the flesh (Levit. 17:14).

Isn't that interesting? Your (human) spirit, the **real you** is located in your soul or soulish area, and before you were converted to Jesus Christ, was drowning in a sea of sin and death within your soul (Rom. 5:12, Eph. 2:1) where all your emotions are sourced.

Your soul or soulish area, however, is located in your BLOOD, which explains why various emotions such as love, hate, and fear etc., affect your blood circulation and makes your heart beat faster or even miss a beat occasionally. Please check the scripture references carefully, and especially any footnotes in your Bible which give the literal Hebrew.

Physical blood gives life to the physical, but the soul **IN** the blood gives life in the spiritual realm and contains man's human spirit.[1] It is therefore true that healing of the flesh will very often include deliverance (observed or unobserved) and the reverse may also be true where soulish problems have manifested themselves in the flesh; that is, deliverance of the soul may result in physical healings, whether quickly or slowly.

1 More fully discussed in *Your Full Salvation*

So far we have introduced **love, sanctification, the Word of God — preaching, healing** (including prayer and fasting) and **deliverance** as possible solutions to the problem of the demonized Christian. With the addition of **praise (worship)** I think we have a complete list of possible BIBLICAL ministries. If we add to these the SECULAR ministry of **medicine (psychiatry)** and examine each solution briefly — but, I hope, accurately — we should be able to arrive at some conclusions which will satisfy, or at least challenge the heart of the Christian who trusts the Bible as the Word of God for today.

1. Preaching.

There can be no doubt that the powerful, anointed preaching of God's Word not only stirs up unclean spirits, but is often effective in driving SOME out. Preachers have often seen people who cannot stop fidgeting during a sermon; others will become drowsy and even fall asleep, and yet others will yawn constantly. These latter symptoms are not necessarily the evidence of a boring sermon, but may be just the reverse. The power of God will very often descend on a congregation when a powerful word is preached and the drowsiness of the hearers can be a combination of this power and the reaction of demons. Yawning is a very common method of the departure of unclean spirits; and, in addition, certain spirits have the character of sending a person to sleep in order to shut their ears from hearing the message.

John Wesley's experience confirms that simple, yet powerfully anointed preaching can have a dynamic effect on demonised people, viz:

> "One before me dropped as dead, and presently a second, and a third. Five others sunk down in half an hour, most of whom were in violent agonies".

> Wesley's Journal, 22nd June, 1739.

"Some sunk down and there remained no strength in them: others exceedingly trembled and quaked: some were torn by a kind of convulsion in every part of their bodies, and that so violently that four or five persons could not hold one of them."

Wesley's Journal, 15th June,1739.

One can imagine Wesley's consternation at the drama taking place during his preaching. What was he to do? It seems perhaps incredible that a scholar of his repute failed to understand at least some of these incidents in terms of the drama surrounding Jesus' public ministry (Mark 1:26,9:18–20, Luke 4:35, 9:39–42), and also that of the apostles (Acts 8:7). One can easily understand his concern at people falling around him as if dead, not realising the power of God at work in many and various ways (cf. Paul's conversion testimony, Acts 26:12–14: also Matt. 28:4, John 18:6, Acts 8:17–18, Rev. 1:17). God's Spirit fell with power upon men, removing their ability to stand before Him. He brought them to the ground to deal with them, but this is far less clearly defined in scripture in comparison with deliverance, the occasional drama of which is plainly recorded.

Whitefield also was troubled and took issue with Wesley over the matter:

"I had an opportunity to talk with him (Whitefield) of those outward signs which had so often accompanied the inward work of God. I found his objections were chiefly grounded on gross misrepresentations of matter of fact. But the next day he had an opportunity of informing himself better: for no sooner had he begun (in the application of his sermon) to invite all sinners to believe in Christ, than four persons sank down close to him, almost in the same moment. One of them lay without either sense or motion. A second trembled exceedingly. The third had strong convulsions all over his body, but made no noise unless by groans. The fourth, equally convulsed, called upon God with strong cries and tears. **From this time, I trust, we shall all suffer God to carry on His own work in the way that pleaseth Him.**"

Wesley's Journal, 7th July, 1739.

May we all learn from the infinite wisdom of Wesley's last remark (cf. Journal entries – April 17, 26; May 1,12, 21; June 16; July 1, 30 – all 1739).

As well as Wesley, another "simple" preacher during the Evangelical Revival of the 18th Century, was obtaining similar disturbing phenomena during preaching. He was **John Berridge** of Everton and the following brief extract is from Balleine's History of the Evangelical Party, pp.78–80:

"... as the people began to grasp the great facts of eternity, there came a terrible epidemic of those hysterical seizures which had accompanied the earlier preaching of Wesley. The same eye-witness describes a typical scene. The sermon had hardly begun, when 'a mixture of various sounds' arose from the congregation, some shrieking, some roaring aloud; the most general was a loud breathing, like that of people half strangled and gasping for life. Others fell down as dead, some in silence, some with extreme noise. An able-bodied, fresh, healthy country-man dropped with a violence inconceivable. I heard the stamping of his feet, ready to break the boards, as he lay in strong convulsions at the bottom of the pew. About the same time John Kelling fell into an agony. Immediately after a well-dressed stranger, who stood facing me, fell backward, wringing his hands and roaring like a bull'. All over the church a perfect Babel of noises broke out; some turned black in the face and gurgled as though they were being choked, some groaned, others yelled, and all the time the deep voice of the preacher quietly went on speaking. And yet Berridge's sermons were far from sensational; there were no Jonathan Edwards' pictures of the terrors of Hell; his own expression that he 'prattled of Jesus' accurately describes his preaching; but **week after week his congregation was transformed into a company of howling maniacs**, and the strange thing was that the men were more subject to these seizures than the women. No one was more astonished than the preacher himself; but with simple faith he decided that this must come either from God or the devil. If it was God, he need not mind, for it would result in good. On the other hand, if it was a device of the devil to try to stop God's work, he must press steadily on".

So much for the positive effects of preaching. In view of the foregoing, I would like to make the following observations which I know to be true from personal experience, regarding the LIMITATIONS of preaching.

(i) **Academic presentation of God's Word achieves little** — the demons flee at the preaching of Jesus' shed blood, death and resurrection, for we preach "not in plausible words of wisdom but in the demonstration of the Spirit and power" (1 Cor. 2:4). Doubts about Wesley's and Berridge's experiences being the manifestation of unclean spirits can be resolved by attending Evangelistic and Deliverance meetings where similar phenomena are observable today.

(ii) The power of God bringing men and women to the ground **is not in itself** evidence that deliverance is taking place, although it is true that a person under the power of God is certainly **rendered ready by the Lord** to be ministered to. We will have more to say about the Power of God later on.

(iii) Likewise, **manifestations** of unclean spirits which wail or shake etc. etc., **are no guarantee that successful deliverance has taken place**. Preaching may well stir up kingdoms of darkness within souls but there may be a great difference between spirits manifesting in order to distract from the preaching, and spirits departing, never to return.

(iv) Preaching may DISTURB ruling-class spirits — it may remove worker-class spirits and it may be strongly supportive of deliverance but let us note its limitations:

(a) **it rarely removes ruler-spirits** (rulers and authorities);

(b) **it can never take the place of direct, anointed ministry.**

You have heard it said, "Preach the Word — that'll get 'em!" What an appealing argument! Preachers love to preach the Word more than anything else and the Word must have primacy in any well-balanced ministry, I gladly agree. It is BECAUSE we love the Word so much that we turn to the Word in order to find our answers. What do we find? We see Jesus teaching in the synagogue and suddenly there is a man with an unclean spirit. What does Jesus do? The easy way is to continue teaching IF that would have the desired and best effect, but we are told that Jesus CEASED TEACHING AND APPLIED THE MINISTRY OF DELIVERANCE DIRECTLY AT THE ENEMY for an authoritative victory. In fact the ministry of deliverance sealed and confirmed the ministry of the Word to the amazement of all present (Mark 1:21–29).

Such incidents are recorded in several places within God's Word, and **it is the Word which tells us WHAT to do and HOW**

to do it — without it we would not know where to start. The Word of God is the sword of the Spirit, but if we only pick up a Bible and start reading it, all we have done (in the area of deliverance) is to buckle this sword around our waist. When we DO what it tells us to do, the sword of God is no longer in its scabbard dangling at our side — it is in our hand! It is being thrust into the darkness and putting the enemy to flight!

Beware of the leaven of the Pharisees in this matter. They were always trumpeting about the Word of God and their submission — in theory — to it. They set themselves up as teachers and loved to tell people what to do (cf. 1 Cor. 4:20), exercising their considerable intellectual talents in explaining away the Word and substituting their own traditions (Mark 7:1–13).

We need to believe and apply (be DOERS of) the Word as well as preach it. We do not have an "either-or" situation here but a "both-and" situation. We should both preach AND apply the Word. As the famous Bible commentator, **Matthew Henry,** in commenting on Mark 1, verse 27, declared, "The design of Christ's gospel is to expel unclean spirits out of the souls of people — 'Come out of the man thou unclean spirit that the Holy Spirit may enter, may take possession of the heart and have dominion in it'".

2. Sanctification.

There can be little doubt that sanctification through the Word of God and prayer will continue to eliminate some unclean spirits from the hearts of Christians (1 Thess. 4:1–8, 2 Cor. 3:18, Rom. 12:1–2), enabling them to overcome such hindrances as fear, rages, deceit, lust etc., as well as bondages to the occult.

However, it ought to be said that sanctification can take place **while unclean spirits remain** within the soul. That is to say, a person can grow more and more like Jesus and exhibit the Fruit of the Spirit simply by controlling, overruling or "putting down" the darkness within them, and walking in the Spirit. We CAN control our unclean spirits, with God's help, if we really want to, and as we grow more like Jesus and increase in His Holy Spirit, so we can overrule them so that we don't even know they are there, most of the time. Sanctification is more likely to help us **control rather than eliminate** them. Many Christians settle for this, but with the Rapture fast approaching and Christ returning for a Bride without spot or blemish, I don't think any Christian can afford to have 5th columnists still residing within God's Temple. Again, don't be fooled by the "either-or" argument. Sanctification AND deliverance are both in God's plan for the Christian. Generally speaking, **sanctification may control** them, but **deliverance** REMOVES them.

These comments, of course, apply to the normal method of sanctification used by the Church to date, contrasting them with the Deliverance Ministry. However it must be obvious that **deliverance should not be considered an ALTERNATIVE to sanctification but a major weapon to be used FOR the sanctifying of the growing Christian.**

Somehow, we have to get across to the Body of Christ the message that deliverance ministry is not just a spectactular extra added onto an evangelistic meeting in order to impress the ignorant with the reality of the risen Lord, although that is quite legitimate. It has an even more important function for the informed people of God in the ongoing life and development of the Church.

Do I hear someone saying that you want a scripture reference before you accept this idea? Please refer to Matthew 15:21–28 where two central points emerge from the story of the deliverance of the Canaanite woman's daughter:

(i)   **Deliverance is for God's Covenantal people FIRST,** and then available for NON-COVENANTAL people IF they manifest faith in the Lordship of Jesus.

(ii) Jesus, who is the Living Bread, describes the deliverance ministry He is being asked to perform **as BREAD — that is, as essential to the people of God as their daily physical bread.**

The I.V.F. Bible Dictionary tells us that the word '**sanctify**' comes from the Latin 'to make holy' and the Hebrew 'to set apart' or 'brightness'. This latter meaning may seem strange to us but the Dictionary goes on to say that "brightness may underlie those usages which relate to condition, state, or process, leading on in the New Testament to the thought of **an inward transformation gradually taking place, resulting in purity**, moral rectitude, and holy, spiritual thoughts expressing themselves in an outward life of goodness and godliness."

The Deliverance ministry is also for the achieving of an **inward transformation, gradually taking place, resulting in purity**. In other words its main use ought to be for the inner cleansing and transformation of **every Christian**, that is, **for our sanctification** (Eph. 5:25–27), and by the time this series of books is completed I think you will agree with me that **the Deliverance Ministry is an essential part of the spiritual weaponry that God has supplied in order to achieve the sanctifying of His people.**

3. Healing

While the scriptures do not appear to lay down a rigid spiritual law in the matter, nevertheless **there is a clear priority for Deliverance prior to Healing in order of ministry.**

I think it is true to say that most of us in the Renewal movement who minister deliverance began with the Lord encouraging us into the Healing ministry first. It was inevitable that we would eventually come up against unclean spirits and we then had the choice of expanding our area of service to include deliverance work or settling for the limitations of ministering only to the flesh of sufferers. Consequently we normally speak today of "Healing and Deliverance", in that order.

However when we turn to the Word of God the emphasis is "Deliverance and Healing". For example the Lord Jesus commissioned His disciples to exercise "authority over unclean spirits so as to cast them out (**first**) and to heal every disease and every illness" (Matt. 10:1).

The daughter of Abraham was **first** loosed from her infirmity (v. 12) — the spirit of infirmity (v.11) — before she was healed (v.13) — (Luke 13:10–17), and a study of a range of scriptures (Matt. 8:16–17, Luke 9:1, 42, Eph. 6:12, 2 Cor. 10:3–5) supports this priority.

Why?

As I have already indicated, many people experience healings which, unbeknown to them, included a deliverance. If a sickness or physical affliction has been caused by a RESIDENT spirit, a messenger of satan sent to buffet you, then a deliverance is necessary to bring about a healing of the flesh. If, however, the causal spirit has departed after afflicting, then the healing ministry is all that is necessary. We hear a lot today about specialised ministries called "healing of the memories" and "healing broken hearts" etc., and we need to ask ourselves if these are physical or spiritual problems. They are obviously not physical and so by applying our rule of thumb, we exercise deliverance. The results? One hundred percent — even on those who were supposed to have been "healed" previously. The conclusion? Behind many a healing there is the unseen deliverance making the healing possible — we have a gracious Lord indeed!

Prayer and fasting are often entered into for deliverance and/or healing and there can be no question that considerable cleansing from spiritual pollution can be achieved this way. However, **prayer and fasting should be seen as an aid to deliverance and not a substitute for it.**

A well-known evangelist tried prayer and fasting to remove a spiritual bondage for many years, without success, and he fell from grace (Gal. 5:4) for a season. (This brother's magazine also espoused the view that a Christian could not have a demon, so how could he arrive at the full truth about his problem?).

A close friend of his said on National Television, "He tried and tried and tried through prayer and fasting and everything he could do to lick it, and it beat him."

This is supported by the Word of God. When Jesus said that a certain kind (rank) of spirit would not come out but by prayer and fasting it is plain that **He was referring to the PREPARATION of a disciple** for warfare. Jesus Himself, thus fully prepared, used His deliverance ministry to get the victory (Mark 9:25–29, Matt. 17:18–21, full texts).

Prayer and fasting is **wonderful preparation** for both the healing and deliverance ministry, indeed any ministry of Christ's.

4. Praise (Worship).

We sometimes find Christian ministers saying, "Deliverance? Let's not focus our attention on satan — on the negative — let's look to Jesus — worship Him — praise Him — that's the way to get delivered!" Can you see how cunningly appealing this view is? Of course we love to praise and worship the Lord, and of course satan hates this. Sometimes it even gets rid of a few worker-class spirits (the expendables). The problem is that this approach is basically unscriptural! *Nowhere in the New Testament did Christ or the apostles organise a praise and worship session ALONE in order to obtain deliverance.* Praise and worship may DISTURB ruling-class spirits; it may be strongly SUPPORTIVE of deliverance and even remove weaker spirits; but it can never TAKE THE PLACE of direct, dynamic anointed ministry. Again, we have a "BOTH-AND" situation. I believe that the best solution is to have the ministry of deliverance IN THE CONTEXT OF the Word of God, and praise, where possible. Where praise and worship support a deliverance ministry, the **DELIVERANCE MINISTER SHOULD CONTROL THE MUSIC ETC.,** but we will say more about this in Book 2.

5. Medicine.

Modern day methods of help extended towards disturbed Christians tend to lean very heavily on psychiatry. The tragic English case of Michael Taylor who brutally murdered his wife after receiving deliverance ministry has led to widespread comment about the need to obtain medical advice (which those ministering endeavoured to obtain without success). Many pertinent questions arise:

1. **Is there TIME** to arrange full medical advice and testing? Usually there is not.

2. Has the subject **financial MEANS** to afford a series of tests? Their condition often coincides with unemployment.

3. In a clear case of a demonised Christian, to "pass the buck" to a psychiatrist is far too facile an answer. **Has the psychiatrist a Christian understanding of demonology?**

4. What effect will **drugs** have on demonization?

5. Will they cure or will they sedate? If only sedation is achieved when and **how are the demons to be removed?**

6. Will highly controversial **shock treatment** be used?

7. Will **occult powers** such as **hypnosis** be used?

These questions highlight the need for biblical psychiatry[1] else the "cure" may well be worse than the infirmity. If the Taylor case has done nothing else, perhaps it has awakened both ministers and psychiatrists to reexamine their methods of diagnosis, treatment, facilities and cooperation; and perhaps the protection afforded them against lawsuits and the sensation seeking media.

6. Deliverance.

We need to remember that the Church's conduct of its ministry should be guided not by the understanding (or lack of it) of the age in which it lives, but rather by the eternal Word of God as revealed in the New Testament. We dare not stray from the guidelines of the New Testament for to do so is to court disaster in a confused world of shifting sand. It is important therefore, in establishing theological principles and patterns for a deliverance ministry not to set up traditions contrary or unknown to the Word of God. Symbolism such as crucifixes and "holy" water etc. are unnecessary, and are more fitting to the superstitious application of occult exorcism. Deliverance is not a magical ritual where the repetitive use of certain formulae gains success. **It is the invoking of the authority and power of the Godhead in the Name of our Lord Jesus Christ against the powers of darkness,** and an understanding of the principles in this series of publications is necessary if Christian leaders are going to be able to use this special Ministry the way God wants it used — TODAY.

It is now my great pleasure to briefly share with you some of the scriptures that I have treasured as foundation stones in presenting the vital importance of this precious ministry. Hopefully they will, by God's grace, inspire you as they have inspired Verlie and myself.

---

1 In my view, a biblical psychiatrist may be described as one who, upon hearing a patient genuinely complain of hearing voices, diagnoses demonization and therefore prescribes deliverance ministry.

When the genuine Christian comes to realise that Deliverance Minsitry is:

(i)   a SALVATION ministry and part of the Saviourhood of the Lord Jesus Christ.

(ii)   established by the Sacrifice of the Cross.

(iii)   referred to as a "top" gift by the Lord.

(iv)   a demonstration of God's cleansing power and the Kingdom of God.

(v)   a test of true and false Christians.

(vi)   FIRST and foremost a BREAD (essential) ministry for God's Covenantal people, that is, the Body of Christ today.

(vii)   COMMANDED by the Lord to be exercised by the Church of God until the close of the New Testament Age in what is known as the Great Commission to the Church.

— and these truths are received into our spirit as well as into our mind, it is virtually impossible to be the same person as we were before, ever again, — no matter how noble and productive our ministry may have been in the past.

We have just made some very bold claims for the Deliverance Ministry of Christ today. Let us begin to supply the scriptures for these **seven foundations**:

(i) Deliverance is a Salvation Ministry

There are several words in the New Testament of our Lord Jesus Christ which are translated by the English word 'heal'. One of them gives us our word 'therapy', another gives us 'hygiene', and. yet another is included in our English word 'psychiatrist'. Why then does Luke, who was himself a physician, describe the man who had a Legion of unclean spirits cast out of him by the Lord as being SAVED?

Dr. Luke had plenty of other words to choose from but he elected to write:

> "And those who had seen (the deliverance) reported to them how the demonised (man) was SAVED"[1]
>
> Luke 8:36 literal

Other healings where Luke prefers to use the word "saved" include the woman who was healed (saved) from continuous bleeding (Luke 8:48). Likewise the tenth leper (the Samaritan) who returned to thank the Lord is described as **saved** (Luke 17:19 lit.) and also the cripple at Lystra (Acts 14:9). These scriptures indicate the Bible teaches that both the deliverance and healing ministries **are salvation ministries** and flow from the Saviourhood of our Lord Jesus Christ.

Actually deliverance and healing are so closely related that the healing of the daughter of Abraham with the crippled spine was achieved by first dealing with the spirit of infirmity (Luke 13:11). How does one deal with a spirit of infirmity? Surely no serious Bible student believes that the Lord would have let that foul spirit stay in the daughter of Abraham during His minstry to her? The discernment of the spirit of infirmity is clearly part of the diagnosis of the problem — indeed the root cause. The Lord's declaration,

> "Woman, you have been LOOSED from your infirmity"
>
> v.12 lit

is clearly **a deliverance command** which is followed by the laying-on-of-hands for **physical restoration** (v.13).

---

1 See also comments on page 24.

One might argue that the cripple at Lystra was saved for eternal life through the ministry of the apostle Paul and we would not deny that. We see no problem with the view that this man received a full salvation from the Lord, both spiritual and physical, because, as the scripture says:

> **"This man heard Paul speaking, who, looking intently at him and seeing that he had faith to be SAVED, said in a loud voice 'Stand upright on your feet!' And he leaped up and walked."**
>
> Acts 14:9–10

The bottom line is that **evangelism, deliverance and healing are all SALVATION MINISTRIES** provided through the Saviourhood of our Lord Jesus Christ (1 John 3:8).

(ii) Deliverance is Established by the Cross of Jesus

There is nothing new about this. Sometimes we Christians who are in the Holy Spirit Renewal movement of this century are pleasantly surprised when we discover that our blessings have been glimpsed by Christians of a previous generation, indeed more than a hundred years ago.

The famous hymn "What a Friend we have in Jesus" was written in 1855 AD by Joseph Scriven. Do you remember how the second line goes?

"All our sins and GRIEFS (SICKNESS) to bear."

Perhaps it meant a lot more to the writer than to many others at the time because he knew quite a lot about grief AND sickness.

In any case we have a sure Word from the Lord in this matter. All we need to do is accept the testimony of Matthew:

> **"When evening came they brought to Him MANY DEMONISED, and he expelled the spirits with a word, and He healed all those with illnesses, so**

that that which was spoken through Isaiah the prophet who said 'He took our infirmities and bore our diseases' was fulfilled"

Matt. 8:16–17 lit.

One cannot have the truth spelled out much clearer than that. When Matthew links the substitutionary atonement of the Messiah from Isaiah 53:4–6 with Jesus' ministry of deliverance (first) and healing he makes it clear that Jesus' **SIN-BEARING, SICKNESS-BEARING** and **PAIN-BEARING**, legally established in Isaiah (check the literal Hebrew in your Bible footnotes), is put into practical effect in the New Testament — even before the Victory of the Cross is physically completed.

Not only that, but that great Victory and Sacrifice is expressed through the deliverance and healing ministries — Matthew says so!

(iii) Deliverance is a Leading Gift

Many people who are searching for some scriptural weapon to use against a deliverance ministry are quick to refer to Jesus' rejection of certain leaders whom He never knew, in spite of their apparently mighty ministries performed in His Name (Matt. 7:19–23).

Even a quick look at Jesus' teaching in this passage will reveal that:

a) The Lord is NOT referring to CHRISTIAN ministries. They may use His Name but HE HAS NEVER KNOWN THEM. He is plainly referring to unregenerate men and women who have never given their lives to Him. No soundly converted Christian need be troubled by this passage.

b) The Lord is emphasising that it is by our FRUITS and not

our MINISTRIES that a CHRISTIAN LEADER should be assessed. He is saying that **even if one sees precious and mighty gifts being used — the top gifts — such as prophecy, deliverance and miracles being exercised**, this does not guarantee or necessarily mean that such a leader is one of the Lord's people. The only criteria are the FRUIT of Christ's character flowing from the new creature and new heart in the leader.

(iv) Deliverance Demonstrates God's Power and Kingdom

There is a very important incident in the Bible where the healing (literal — therapy) of a blind and dumb demoniac (demonised man — Matt. 12:22) triggers a severe clash with religious leaders especially sent down from Jerusalem to cut this young (and dangerous) Rabbi, Jesus, down to size (Mark 3:22).

I thank God for this incident and Jesus' response to his accusers. It produces some of the richest teaching about spiritual warfare in the whole of the Bible (Matt. 12), and we will certainly be looking at this again within the Christian Deliverance series of books[1]. However, one statement of the Lord's stands out above all the others. Jesus said,

> **"If I by the Spirit of God cast out demons, then is the Kingdom of God come upon you."**
> Matt. 12:28

— or if you prefer Luke's account, it is by the FINGER of God (Luke 11:20 cf. Exodus 31:18). It is apparent that the Spirit of God is the Finger of God and that the Kingdom of God means the Rule of God. That is to say, **the Rule of God has displaced the rule of satan whenever demons are cast out by the Holy Spirit.**

What a glorious description and vindication of the deliverance

---

1 Book 3 *Walking in Victory*, Chap. 8, 2(ii).

ministry are these words of the Lord!

How wonderful it is to know that the Kingdom or Rule of God in and over the human **heart, SOUL, MIND and BODY** obviously increases step by step as **unclean** spirits are cast out and the **HOLY** Spirit prayed in.

This infers a progressive growth in the Kingdom of God (cf. Mark 4:28–32) and is clearly the teaching of the context of the passage in Matthew. That is, the blind and dumb demoniac was healed (therapied), which confirms this fourth foundation point that deliverance is a demonstration of God's cleansing power, and it is also a demonstration of the Kingdom (Rule) of God.

(v) Deliverance Exposes True and False Christians

> "Or how can one enter a strong (man's) house and plunder his vessels, unless he first binds the strong? Then indeed he may plunder his house. He who is not with me is against me, and he who does not gather with me scatters."
>
> Matt 12:29–30

Jesus spoke the above words in the context of the **dramatic healing and deliverance of a blind and dumb demoniac**. Satan had expanded his kingdom or rule in the unfortunate person to include blindness and dumbness, but not for long. What a mighty Saviour and Lord we have!

The Christian cannot sit on the fence regarding Christ's deliverance ministry — it will sort you out — HE will sort you out and shake you like you have never been sorted out and shaken before. You say you are a Christian? You say you have fully committed your life to Christ whatever the cost? Then you dare not make a mistake about your assessment of a deliverance ministry! Because if it is Christ's, then the Kingdom of God is right there and you cannot even stand by neutrally. **You must be**

committed to support that work of His Spirit at least morally, for IF YOU ARE NOT WITH HIM YOU ARE AGAINST HIM. Do you believe this? Let me say it again, **IF YOU ARE NOT WITH HIM YOU ARE AGAINST HIM!** It is the plain meaning of Jesus' words. All the verbiage about being a disciple, believing God's Word, being a son of the Reformation, an evangelical or a Pentecostal or a Catholic or this or that etc. IS JUST SO MUCH WORTHLESS HOT AIR unless you can stand with Christ in His deliverance work and say "I am with you Lord!" Amen? Hallelujah!

Being able to do this, Jesus says, qualifies YOU as a gatherer with Him and being unable to do this makes YOU a scatterer, that is, GATHERING FOR the Kingdom of God or SCATTERING FROM the Kingdom of God — a sheep or a wolf! When the Lord warned us of wolves in sheep's clothing He surely meant to warn us not to be deceived by the APPEARANCE of "Christians" but to observe whether or not they bore good fruit or taught destructive heresies (Matt. 7:15, 2 Peter 2:1–2).

Where do YOU stand in this matter?

(vi) Deliverance is BREAD (essential) for God's people

This has been discussed earlier under the heading of SANCTIFICATION but perhaps we should dwell on this wonderful principle a moment longer. Jesus Himself said that He was the Living Bread who gives Life to the World (John 6:32–35, 47–48, 51) and for Jesus to declare that Deliverance is a Bread ministry is a high ranking indeed.

We now have two propositions which need weighing:

(i) Jesus is the (Living) Bread
(ii) Deliverance is a Bread ministry

— from which I think it is fair to say that when the Lord

ministers Deliverance to a sufferer **He is GIVING HIMSELF, just as He did on the Cross, as the Bread of Life.**

Let us stop right here for a moment — doesn't that just boggle your mind?

When we add yet another scriptural proposition, that (iii) **when demons are cast out by the Spirit of God the Kingdom of God comes upon the sufferer** (Matt. 12:28), we begin to understand why the enemy bends every effort to hinder and block the ministry from touching human lives. I find it difficult to grasp the magnitude, the full spiritual magnitude, of these mind-blowing statements in the Word of God about the Deliverance Ministry of the Lord Jesus Christ.

We will refer to this principle again in Book 2, Chapter 6, 1 (iv) in more detail.

(vii) Deliverance is Commanded for Today

Very simply, the Lord Jesus commanded His disciples to cast out demons (among other things) and gave them TOTAL authority to carry out this command:

> "... gave them authority over unclean spirits so as to cast them out, and to heal EVERY DISEASE and EVERY ILLNESS"
>
> Matt. 10:1 cf. Luke 9:1

Please note, this two-fold ministry authority is for casting out demons FIRST, because only then can EVERY disease and EVERY illness be overcome. The emphasis is the same as Matt. 8:16–17 and Luke 13:12–13 (see section (i)). How can one ALWAYS obtain physical healing UNLESS the battle is won in the spiritual realm FIRST? (Eph. 6:12, 2 Cor. 10:3–5). Praise the Lord for His mighty provision for the needs of His people!

It is important to realise that this powerful two-edged authority has never been retracted. Some commands of the Lord in the New

Testament may have been retracted later (Luke 22:35–38), BUT NOT THIS ONE! On the contrary, the Great Commission of our Lord Jesus Christ clearly demands that this authority be taught to ALL new disciples in succeeding generations, right through to the close of the New Testament Age:

> "Go, therefore, and disciple the nations, baptizing them ... TEACHING THEM TO KEEP STRICTLY (GUARD, PRESERVE) EVERYTHING WHATEVER I COMMANDED YOU"
>
> Matt. 28:19–20 lit.

This forceful emphasis by the Lord for the need for the continuity of teaching His commands to future disciples can hardly be made more strongly or more clearly. The Great Commission is quite rightly considered by Christians everywhere as a command. Unfortunately deliverance and healing are part of the instruction that the world-wide Church has either failed to perceive, ignored or shrunk from ministering — until now. We have, for the most part, been quite unaware that we have been keeping some of the children's Bread from them.

7. Summary

Some of these **seven (7) major foundations of Deliverance Ministry** will be discussed again in this series of books on Deliverance, but we trust that we have, by the grace of God, been able to lay for you a solid foundation on which to build your own ministry for His glory, if He so leads you, or your colleagues.

Every ministry has its rightful place in the sovereign plan and provision of God. They are all complementary to each other and may overlap considerably in the building of God's Kingdom. But never let us forget that if preaching, or praise, or sanctification, or healing, or medicine, or all of them put together could remove all the kingdoms of darkness from the human soul, then Jesus would never have needed to command, "Come out of him, and enter him no more!" All the cowardice and cleverness of men seeking an easier alternative solution will perish on the Rock of the Word of Jesus Christ.

Let us remember then, that **the classical biblical solution to demonization is the ministry of deliverance.** Other ministries may substitute or suffice from time to time but that is more by the grace of Christ and the presence of Christ rather than the spiritual wisdom of the Church.

It is a ministry of LOVE, because it is the love of Christ for the sufferer — in you — that motivates the Christian leader to go into battle, when it would be so much easier to apply some or all of the other possible solutions — hoping for the best. But to get the best results, you have to apply the best provision or gift that God has given you for meeting the needs of His people.

Do you love them enough?

3

PREPARATION OF THE MINISTER

There are a number of areas that a responsible Christian will need to study carefully if he or she is desirous of being used by the Lord in deliverance work. We discuss these below and, while we have tried to keep the discussions brief regarding the better known subjects, they are ALL regarded as important.

1. Who May Cast Out?

To phrase this another way we could ask ourselves, "**Who has the AUTHORITY to cast out?**" Authority is the basis of all successful Christian activity. To illustrate from secular life, a traffic policeman is given authority to direct road traffic by the community which he serves. He has an authority (to be used responsibly) over and above that of ordinary citizens, and together with that **authority** he has been given the **power** to arrest and charge those persons who fail to obey his authority. Thus, for law and order to operate, we separate a man from our midst and (first) give him **authority** to police our road laws, and (second) we give him the **power** to ensure that his authority stands up under pressure and he can get the job done. The power gives him "teeth" against the rebellious. It is utterly useless (and we see this all around us today) giving people authority to do a job if we don't also give them the power to carry it out against opposing pressures; otherwise they only become "meat in the sandwich". It is also essential we remember that when a person is given authority and that authority is challenged, it is in effect a challenge on the GIVER (in this case the State Government) rather than on the giver's delegate (the policeman).

Let us now look at the chain of authority from our Lord Jesus Christ to YOU.

- And He (Jesus) called to Him His twelve disciples and gave them AUTHORITY over unclean spirits, to cast them out, and to heal every disease and every infirmity".

  Matt. 10:1

- "He gave them (the twelve) AUTHORITY over all the demons ..."

  Luke 9:1–2

- "I have given you (seventy) AUTHORITY ... over all the power of the enemy: and nothing shall hurt you".

  Luke 10:19

- "ALL AUTHORITY in heaven and on the earth has been given to me. Go therefore and make disciples of all nations ... teaching them to observe (guard, preserve, keep strictly) all that I have commanded you; and lo, I am with you always, to the close of the age".

  Matt.28:19–20

- "All things are possible to him who believes ... "

  Mark 9:23

- "Truly, truly, I say to you, he who believes in me will also do the works that I do ..."

  John 14:12

- "And these signs will accompany those who believe; in My Name they will cast out demons ..."

  Mark 16:17

Here we have a few select verses which convey to us that Jesus' authority is passed on to his twelve disciples, and also to the seventy disciples. **But it doesn't stop there.** The twelve are to "disciple all the nations" and **the gospel traditions are to be carried down (strictly) by the new disciples through all generations to the close of the Age.**

We are in the tradition of those following-on disciples who have been baptised among the nations and in due course, as we go on to heavenly glory, there will be other disciples raised up by the Holy Spirit to serve Christ. Each generation of disciples is to guard, keep strictly, preserve, all that Christ has commanded the early ones. You can't get it any clearer than that. It is an ongoing authoritative chain, not of ecclesiastical orders as some people sometimes think, **but it is an authoritative chain of ministry to and through disciples.** Now you say, "What do you mean by 'disciples', Peter?" Well, I mean those who believe. As Jesus said:

> "All things are possible to him who believes". "Truly, truly, I say unto you, he who believes in Me will also do the works I do".
>
> " ... and these signs will accompany those who believe. In my Name they will cast out demons ..."

So ANY Christian may aspire to the Ministry of Deliverance PROVIDED such aspirations are from the Holy Spirit.

Let us be encouraged by reminding ourselves that the disciples were not very clever. They had not received the formal education that you and I have had. They were constantly being chided by Jesus for their slowness to understand. Jesus said to them, "Do you not yet understand?" and there were times in His ministry when they would not approach Him to ask a question. They were dull and could not understand Him, and they were afraid to ask Him because they feared He would chide them again. They were ordinary men — some of them fishermen, as you know; others with ordinary jobs, chosen from the stuff of the earth of the Middle East. It was to these men Jesus said, "I give you authority, go and preach the Gospel of the Kingdom, heal the sick, cast out demons ... etc." **It is something which any child of God can do.**

Now, when did Jesus teach them to do this? He taught them in the very earliest stages of their training. He didn't wait till they had their diploma or degree, or perhaps a Ph.D. At the very beginning, in the first eighteen months of their training, he sent them out on missions to the villages and towns WITH HIS AUTHORITY and I reckon that if they could do it, any disciple could do it — by faith and by the power of God.

Who may cast out? You may, according to God's Word.[1] One thing more needs to be said. We certainly have authority to minister in those areas where the Word of God states this quite clearly, but we want to avoid the error of thinking that God MUST back up whatever we command because Jesus said: "Whatever you bind on earth shall be bound in heaven and whatever you loose on earth shall be loosed in heaven" (Matt.18:18).

There are some things to be noted before we can really appreciate the meaning of these words.

Firstly, "You" is plural (you all) so that Jesus certainly meant these words to apply to all the disciples, and therefore to us.

Secondly, "shall be bound" and "shall be loosed" reads literally in the Greek text "shall be *having* been bound" and "shall be *having* been loosed". At first sight Jesus appears to give unlimited authority to His disciples, that heaven in effect will back up their authority unreservedly. However, the peculiar construction of the Greek reveals rather that "what they bind on earth" will be "what **has been** bound" in heaven, and likewise with loosing, This is to say that, as they exercise their discipleship IN ACCORDANCE WITH THE TEACHING OF JESUS (i.e. the New Covenant) and the WILL OF GOD as led by the Holy Spirit, **the things that they**

1 But for qualifying comments see also Book 4 Section "The Minister's Attitude to Himself."

bind and loose will already have been predestined in heaven (Eph. 2:10) and thus power will be supplied to back up our Godly use of authority.[1] There is a big difference between guaranteeing heavenly endorsement for every Christian action on the one hand, and promising that our Holy Spirit inspired actions have been predestined in heaven, on the other.

The crux of the matter is that "those who believe" have the necessary authority, for **belief or trust in Jesus is the basis of discipleship under His Lordship.**

2. The Shield of Faith.

There are a number of things recorded in the scriptures as spiritual weaponry which a Christian might consider essential in warfare against the powers of darkness, and most of them would normally be considered part of everyday walking in the Spirit. For example a Christian should use the truth — what the apostle Paul describes as the girdle of truth. Likewise with the breastplate of righteousness and the sword of the Spirit, etc. The Christian armour as recorded in Ephesians chapter 6:10–17, includes those things that every Christian should daily employ.

We have already discussed authority, which I understand Paul to include in the "**feet** shod with the preparation of the gospel of peace". The Christian's **feet** are so shod that he can tread on serpents and scorpions and over all the power of the enemy (Luke 10:19) — he can crush satan under his **feet** (Rom. 16:20) — and put his feet on the necks of all kinds of filthy, unclean (spiritual) kings and princes (Josh. 10:23–27). Authority is a key weapon and given to Christians by the Word of God, but if there is one other essential piece of armour to explain to you, my choice

---

1 For a fuller treatment of this subject, see our book "Christian Authority and Power."

would have to be **the shield of faith**, because it quenches all the fiery darts of the evil one.

How is this so?

Stated briefly, in prayer, I raise my shield of faith by placing my faith in the blood of Jesus Christ the Passover Lamb sacrificed for me, believing that His blood is a sign to me that God has covenanted not to permit the destroyer to attack my household whilesoever we each keep covenant with Him (i.e. stay under the blood of the Passover covenant). Confused? Well, we need to go back in the Old Testament where it all started in Exodus 12.

Most Christian leaders will be familiar with the story of how the Hebrews were finally released by Pharaoh from their slavery in Egypt. Plague after plague was visited upon the Egyptians but Pharaoh would not let God's people go until the destroyer visited the Egyptians and took the life of the first-born in every household. The destroyer sought out Egyptian families only (v.23) because Moses had instructed the Hebrews to take a lamb sacrifice for each of their households (v.3), and to mark the (outside) doorposts and lintels with the blood of the lamb and to stay in the house until morning (vv.7,22). The lamb was to be eaten within the house; the feast was to be called **the Lord's Passover** (v.11). The scripture goes on to say:

> "For I will go through the land of Egypt in that night, and will smite all the firstborn in the land of Egypt, both man and beast, and against all the gods of Egypt will I execute judgements: I am the LORD. And the blood shall be to you for a token upon the houses where you are, and when I see the blood I will pass over you and there shall be no plague upon you to destroy you, when I smite the land of Egypt."
>
> Exodus 12:12–13

God actually covenanted with the Hebrews that the destroyer

would not be permitted to harm the Hebrew families that had eaten the Passover lamb and **marked their doors with its blood,** and stayed indoors, under the protection of the sign of the blood, all night.

Now we know that Christ fulfilled all the animal sacrifices of the Old Covenant by offering Himself as the Lamb of God without spot or blemish for the sins of the world, but we need to remember that He was not only the SACRIFICIAL Lamb offered for sin but ALSO the PASSOVER Lamb for covering and protection.

Paul specifically refers to Jesus as **our Passover (Lamb) who has been sacrificed** (1 Cor. 5:7), and the New Testament further tells us that we are to have **faith in His blood** (Rom. 3:25 AV) and that we are **guarded/kept by the power of God through FAITH** (1 Peter 1:5).

We don't have any literal blood to splash on our doorposts, because **Christ died ONCE FOR ALL** (Heb. 9:12, 10:10) but —

(i)   **we CAN exercise faith in the victory** of His shed blood at Calvary, not only for sin but for covering;

(ii)   **we CAN claim the promises of God** in this regard, and in prayer raise the shield of faith, e.g., " ... and I raise the shield of faith, which faith is in the blood of Jesus Christ my Passover Lamb sacrificed for me and my house to quench all the fiery darts of the evil one, that we might be kept safe this day by the power of God and the promises of God in all our doings — in our going out and in our coming in — because we are sprinkled with the blood of Jesus, and the destroyer is forced to pass over us..."

– and

(iii)   **we CAN stay under the safety of the blood** by obeying the New Covenant which God has provided to enable us to safely negotiate our way in this wicked world. When we sin, let us confess it quickly, that we might stay under the blood and that the blessing of God's protection may continue to rest upon us and our loved ones over whom we exercise a leadership under the Lordship of Christ.

Two further points may be discussed with profit:

(i)   Although **Job** continually offered sacrifices for himself and his family, he was sorely afflicted due to a conflict between God and satan in heaven (Job 1:1, 2:8). However, this was in the divine will of God and eventually brought great blessing to Job (Job 42:10–end). From all the evidence we might conclude that while satan is generally not permitted to afflict God's people when they are covered, and stay under the precious blood of Christ our Passover Lamb, there may be temporary exceptions due to the secret will of God, and which will be turned into blessing for those who hold fast under pressure (Job 42:10–17, cf. Gen. 50:20, Rom. 8:28, 2 Cor. 2:14, James 1:2–4).

(ii)   Anyone eating the bread or drinking the cup of the Lord unworthily shall be guilty of the body and blood of the Lord, and it is necessary to **discern the body** (of Christ and of believers) otherwise sickness and death may result (1 Cor. 11:27–30). From this I understand that to appreciate the blood rightly and to remember the shed blood with gratitude at the Lord's supper, brings to us and keeps us in the blessings of the New Covenantal relationship with Him; but to profane and abuse the blood and the body (of Christ and of believers) is to open ourselves to judgment and demonic attack.

I don't think there is a day that goes by when I and my family are not covered by Jesus' blood — I certainly hope not, whether deliverance ministry is taking place or not. But if there is deliverance, the prayer for the raising of the shield of faith in His blood is repeated for all those present. **I regard it as absolutely essential**. The shield of faith is basic defence which enables the Christian to press the attack, knowing in your spirit that you have the **AUTHORITY to tread on serpents and scorpions and over ALL the POWER of the enemy, AND NOTHING SHALL (EVER) HURT YOU!** (Luke 10:19).

In the English language a double negative becomes a positive, but in New Testament Greek a double negative becomes a very strong negative. In the above we have a TRIPLE negative which is as emphatic as you can get — "AND NO THING SHALL NOT NOT HURT YOU!" Hallelujah! Thank God for the New Covenant sealed with the blood of Jesus Christ!

It's the old, old story of our Christian faith; **you get what you believe God's Word for**.

3. Forbidding to Minister.

Before we minister, it is helpful to consider the case where the disciples FORBADE ministry:

> "'Master, we saw a man casting out demons in Your Name, and we forbade him because he does not follow with us.' But Jesus said to him, 'Do not forbid him; for he **that is not against you is for you.**'"
>
> Luke 9:49–50, see also Mark 9:38–39

Here we have the disciples taking it upon themselves to forbid the ministry of an unknown. Who can this unknown be? Where did he receive his training? Is his work for the glory of God or does he want glory from men? What is his authority?

None of these questions are answered for us except perhaps we can say that as he exercises his ministry in the name of Jesus, he is using the authority of that Name. Perhaps he has seen the "ordinariness" of the twelve disciples and, believing in Jesus as the Christ, has found himself in an emergency situation where a brother Jew has been tormented by unclean spirits, and a desperate situation required the desperate action of faith.

The crux of the whole matter is that the disciples were quickly on the scene and put a stop to it. Today's Christian leader might respond this way — "Why, this fellow has had no training and no calling by Jesus that I know of! What a nerve! Apart from the fact that it can be dangerous work, didn't he know that one had to be 'ordained' i.e. receive the call from Jesus and have hands laid on him etc. etc. to convey authority and power? What church does he belong to? Whose 'covering' is he under?"

JESUS' RESPONSE TO THEIR REACTION.

Fortunately for us all, the disciples' vision of God's work is far, far too small. Their self-imposed limitations are quickly demolished by the One who came, not to judge but to save. All over the world we find Christians forbidding this and despising that in flat contradiction of the teaching of the Lord and His apostles in the New Testament. *I believe it to be wise to caution and instruct would-be ministers, but it is certainly wrong to forbid or to straight-jacket the ministry in a way which makes it impotent — then only satan can profit.*

I can remember an incident which forced me to practice what I preach. I had been invited to teach a North Shore charismatic assembly and shared with them some fundamentals about soulishness and deliverance. I remember thinking what a spiritually bound up lot they were — bikies, druggies etc., and you can imagine my surprise when one young bikie with the most battered and spiritually bound up face I'd ever seen rang me later and said, "Hey, Peter, we've got one of the girls spaced out on the floor here and we are casting demons out of her. What do we do next?"

I froze in horror and was about to tell them how to wrap it up and then chide them for not having their Pastor's permission or presence with them, when the Holy Spirit convicted me that I would be making the same mistake as the Lord's disciples — limiting the sovereignty of God in an emergency situation. So I guided and cautioned them appropriately and prayed fervently as soon as I was off the phone! Praise the Lord, it all turned out fine and I had cause to reflect again on the goodness of the Lord and the trustworthiness of His living Word, i.e., the written Word of God made alive by His Spirit.

Perhaps the thrust of Jesus' answer lies in the matter of whose side you are on. The spiritual warfare is in deadly earnest, and by definition those who are not against you must be for you (cf. Luke 9:50, 11:23; Matt. 12:30). Those who cast out demons in Jesus' name can GENERALLY be said to be on the side of Jesus and the disciples, and apparently the opposite also is true, that THOSE WHO FORBID ARE AGAINST HIM.[1] True or false? It appears that our Lord Jesus Christ is just as controversial today (by men's standards) as He was in the New Testament days, but then, is He not the same yesterday, today and forever?

4. Non-Christian Exorcism.

Something ought to be said about non-christian exorcism (as distinct from Christian deliverance). Two scriptures bear examination:

(i) The seven sons of Sceva.

This is a very well-known passage, and yet rarely preached,

---

1 See also Chapter 8, 2. (ii) d. — Book 3 *WALKING IN VICTORY*

and so perhaps we should read it carefully first:

> "Then some of the itinerant Jewish exorcists (*exorkistone*) undertook to pronounce the name of the Lord Jesus over those who had evil spirits, saying, 'I adjure (*orkidso*) you by the Jesus whom Paul preaches'. Seven sons of a Jewish high priest named Sceva were doing this. But the evil spirit answered them, 'Jesus I know, and Paul I know; but who are you?' And the man in whom the evil spirit was leaped on them, mastered both[1] of them, and overpowered them, so that they fled out of the house naked and wounded. And this became known to all the residents of Ephesus, both Jews and Greeks; and fear fell upon them all; and the name of the Lord Jesus was extolled" (Acts 19:13–17).

It is worth noting the following:

1) The unregenerate Jewish exorcists think they can copy Paul's anointed ministry — and a sharp, severe lesson is learned. Although the Name of Jesus is the greatest in Heaven and earth — using the Name as a magic formula on the assumption that power and authority automatically goes with the Name is a serious error. With the Name must go God's call, and ANOINTING OF AUTHORITY AND POWER, and these essentials can only be present when Christ's Word abides within the heart, and is made alive by God's Holy Spirit.

2) The unclean spirit reacts violently to powerless ministry. They know the strengths and weaknesses of those who stand against them far better (unfortunately) than Christians know their enemy. Here is one reason why non-Christians ought not to copy

---

1 The problem of textual interpretation here is best explained by understanding that TWO out of SEVEN exorcists were involved in this incident.

Christian deliverance.

3) Although this calamitous incident has the appearance of a victory for the powers of darkness, in fact it brings a very positive reaction from the residents of Ephesus — the Name of the Lord Jesus was extolled. His ways are certainly not our ways at times!

(ii) Jesus' reaction to non-christian exorcism.

> "A sound tree cannot bear evil fruit, nor can a bad tree bear good fruit. Every tree that does not bear good fruit is cut down and thrown into the fire. Thus you will know them by their fruits .... On that day many will say to me, 'Lord, Lord, did we not prophesy in your name, and **cast out demons in your name**, and do many mighty works in your name?' And then will I declare to them, 'I never knew you; depart from me, you evildoers.'"
>
> Matt. 7:18–20, 22–23 RSV

As we have seen before, this passage does NOT refer to soundly converted Christians, for the Lord said "I NEVER KNEW YOU!" Here the Lord Jesus warns that even if pagan or occult ministries such as carried out by witch-doctors, spiritists, hypnotists and various sundry methods are successful in removing unclean spirits — and even if performed in Jesus' name — that does not guarantee that the ministry is of the Lord, or the ministers belong to the Lord and are members of the Kingdom of God.

Occultists can cast out demons. They do it in an appeasing kind of way by offering sacrifices, negotiating and cajoling and making deals with spirits. Their methods are nothing like the authoritative way of Christ and the Apostles, but nevertheless they can do that kind of thing. The Pharisees and scribes from Jerusalem knew this basic principle; hence they had no hesitation in saying that Jesus cast out demons by Beelzebub, thus getting themselves in a lot of trouble. We will discuss that charge further in Book 3, Chapter 8, entitled "Opposition".

There are at **least three (3) check points** that Christians can apply to ANY ministry in order to test for validity or counterfeiting. They are:

(i)   Is the ministry based on scriptural PRINCIPLES? (Not necessarily methods, because methods can change but principles rarely do.)

(ii) Does the ministry give and bring GLORY to Christ?

(iii) Does the ministry show forth the fruit of the Spirit THROUGH ITS MINISTERS, and eventually through those being ministered to?

Sometimes people who do not understand how deliverance works look for the fruit of the Spirit to show forth in the lives of people who are in the process of getting rid of unclean spirits. Not realising the continuity of the battle, they expect the fruit of the Spirit to show forth in a matter of weeks. I want to say loud and clear that people who are in the midst of prolonged battle will rarely be able to consistently show such fruit. When the battle is OVER and they have WON, then they can rejoice in the fulness of the Holy Spirit. **If you want to test a ministry for fruit you must FIRST look at the MINISTERS** — this is the meaning of Jesus' teaching. Obviously as time goes by the fruit of the Spirit will show forth through their people also, but you must first look for fruit in the lives of the prophets, deliverance ministers. And miracle workers, etc ...

Counterfeiting is more subtle than most Christians think — it has to be or it is a waste of time. If I were to draw a copy of a $20 note it wouldn't fool anyone. An artist MIGHT be able to draw a note that would fool ME (a financial layman) but he would not fool a trained Bank officer. No, for a counterfeit to be successful it has to be identical, or almost identical, to the original or it will be quickly exposed. That is why many Christians who also have an unclean religious spirit[1] seem very religious on the one hand, but on the other hand they are unsuccessful in either showing forth the fruit of the Spirit themselves or extending the Kingdom of God in the lives of others. They look good and they sound good, but the work of the religious spirit in them continually nullifies what they are trying to do by the Holy Spirit, and the result? ... **Little or no fruit.**

Please remember that counterfeits are often difficult to perceive but even though counterfeits have to be clever and close to the original to have any chance of deceiving, spiritual perception and discernment will provide the answers for the Christian who knows the Scriptures, and walks in the Spirit, in God's perfect timing.

Beware of endeavouring to use false ministries — such as your own strength (the flesh), and hypnosis or other occult powers. Beware of ministries with fancy names which appear to **combine spiritual and scientific techniques.**[2] Remember that your authority comes from the Word of God. Study the Scriptures and **put your trust wholly in them.**

5. Where to Cast Out (Deliver).

The next thing: Where to cast out? Where to deliver? How is it done? Is it done privately, or publicly? Well, we have to say that there is a great reluctance to minister deliverance in public, and I think that perhaps one reason is sensitivity for the onlookers who may never have seen deliverance before. You

---

1 More fully discussed in Book 4

2 See "The Seduction of Christianity" by Hunt & McMahon.

may worry about offending those who are looking on, who don't really understand; the fear of offending the uninformed; not to mention the possibility of a protracted battle. Some battles can go on for a long time and this may seem unsuitable even for a Christian public meeting. I think the main reason is, however, a conviction that this ministry is a personal and delicate one, perhaps even humiliating to the subject at times, and therefore should be attended to privately. However, **this conviction is apparently not shared by Jesus Christ or the apostles.** I cannot find an incident of deliverance (that is clearly DELIVERANCE) in the Scriptures that was not done publicly. You may reason that there were private HEALINGS. Peter's mother-in-law was sick with a fever and you might like to think of that as a deliverance, and I wouldn't argue with you. There may be other incidents like that where you might say, "Ah, that's a deliverance". That may be so, but the clearest cases of deliverance in the New Testament are always performed publicly, and I believe the reason is that is where the need was. Jesus walked down the street and there would be somebody who needed help. There would be the man bringing the epileptic boy, who was also deaf and dumb, to Him in public, and everybody would be crowding around. The disciples couldn't cast it out and the big crowd was hanging around and murmuring, "Oh, Oh, what has He done! He has killed him!" — when the lad "fainted". One can sense a wave of horror going through the crowd as the spirit dashes the boy down, but, of course, when he is raised, healed, that is a different story. And there are other stories like that; for example, the incident of the deaf and dumb demoniac whom Christ healed in public, in front of the scribes and Pharisees, and they say, "By Beelzebub he casts out demons because he is the prince of demons". All in public, and all with critical eyes gazing on. Jesus had dozens of critical spirits looking on, and so did the apostles, and I believe we just have to minister in whatever circumstances the Lord calls us to minister.

The criterion which really matters is **the need** of the person who comes in desperation and says, "Help me!" — wherever you are. I am not suggesting you start ministering on buses or this kind of thing, but I am suggesting that you may not have the time to take people miles to your home to minister privately; you might have to walk into a park or a local church to minister — or something like that. The interesting thing is that Jesus ministered this way in the synagogue. How is that for asking for trouble? On the Sabbath, as well. That is really taking your life in your hands, isn't it?

Choosing the Battleground

I believe the scripture gives us the clear principle that **a person's need is the paramount consideration**. We don't want to find excuses for NOT ministering, but having said that, it is better if we can surround the sufferer with a circle of faith, away from prying, unbelieving eyes in a building separated for the worship and purposes of God — where time does not matter, and noise can be blotted out either by soundproofing, or praises to God, or both. Soft floor coverings are an advantage in case the sufferer is prostrated by the power of God and the ministry is performed at floor level.

Where to minister? Virtually anywhere — but **use discretion if you have a choice.** The NEEDS of the troubled must always be of prior importance and other circumstances secondary, and this is the example set us by our Lord and the early church.

6. Discerning of Spirits.

Introduction.

The Lord may well quicken the spiritual sensitivity of the Christian leader so that the gift of **discerning of spirits** will operate and open up the true nature of the problems of the sufferer. From the very beginning, we need to know a little about discernment, as it can take place at any time that the minister and the sufferer are "within range" of each other; and, of course, we obtain our fundamental understanding of the gift from the Word of God.

The word translated "**discern**" also means **weigh, judge** or **distinguish (between)** and is essential if we are to discern what spirits are indwelling the human soul. We know, of course, that we have (1) a human spirit; and also that every Christian is indwelt by (2) the Holy Spirit (Rom. 8:9, 15–16); and (3) that we can receive a spirit of (slavery into) fear, or a different (unclean) spirit from the one we received through the apostolic preaching of Jesus (2 Cor. 11 :4). We are also told that an unclean spirit which breaches our spiritual defences can invite as many as seven other (types of) spirits to join him within a living soul (Matt. 12:45).

Discernment is exercised in the Old Testament; for example, **King Saul** had the Spirit of the Lord come mightily upon him so that he prophesied (1 Sam. 12); then disobeyed God with the result that the Spirit of the Lord departed from Saul and an evil spirit from the Lord tormented him. The Scriptures tell us that Saul's servants (exercising discernment) said to him, "Behold now, an evil spirit from God is tormenting you" (1 Sam. 16:14–15). This was not difficult as Saul was obviously paranoid about David.

Apart from outward appearance, our conversation is a very obvious area requiring or inviting discernment. The New Testament tells us that a person speaking by means of the Holy Spirit cannot say "Jesus be cursed", and no one can say "Jesus is Lord" except by the Holy Spirit (1 Cor.12:3). Thus, when a person blasphemes, you don't win an earthly prize for discerning a spirit of blasphemy — such things are obvious when people converse and reveal their lust, profanity, jealousy, anger, perversity, greed, etc. with every idle word. However, when a prophecy is given in the assembly, its **spiritual** author may not be so easily identified and so discernment is applied, presumably by those qualified to do so (usually the elders and prophets) in the assembly (1 Cor. 14:29, 1 John 4:1–6). This is also true where teaching is concerned, because to receive false teaching is to receive "a different spirit" (1 Tim. 4:1, 2 Cor. 11:4).

(i) Operation.

To underline that the gift of discernment is also used to discern the gift and the working of the Holy Spirit, Paul actually discerned **faith** in a man crippled from birth and "**seeing that he had faith to be made well**, said in a loud voice, 'Stand upright on your feet!' And he sprang up and walked" (Acts 14:8–10) Faith is one of the easier things for Pastors to see in their flock. On the other hand, Paul also perceived that the men of Athens were very **religious**. How did he come to that conclusion? Simply because he couldn't help noticing that the city was full of idols (Acts 17:16, 22). But perhaps even more significant to us who are examining the deliverance ministry is Paul's confrontation and spiritual conflict with Elymas the magician (Acts 13:8–10), and the slave girl (Acts 16:16–18). We need to ask ourselves why Paul **peered intently** at Elymas before pronouncing a judgement (discernment) on him, and why did he deliver the slave girl from the **spirit of a python** (literal Greek) when she appeared to be only proclaiming the truth? Obviously discernment took place in all these incidents, and mighty works followed.

Having looked at some scriptural principles and examples of the gift of discernment, let us now introduce its operation. A deliverance minister may meet people who need deliverance in any situation. You may open your front door in answer to the doorbell and before a word can be spoken, in a split second you will "pick up" in your spirit the "heart" of the person at your door. When I say the "heart" of the person I mean the spirit that dominates them (in their soul), or perhaps the spirit that is manifesting through them at the time. Just as the heart of flesh that God created in us dominates our circulatory system and gives life to the body, the Bible speaks of our **spiritual heart** — that which dominates our complex spiritual system. In the perfect will of God we should be continuously filled with the Holy Spirit, who then exercises His Lordship over our human spirit, and together they rule the soul and the mind and the body to the Glory of God. However, very few of us measure up to this perfect standard because (1) we are not truly and continuously filled with the Holy Spirit and consequently (2) the lusts of the flesh and sin remain to war against the soul and influence us wrongly with varying degrees of success. Now, if the words "spiritual heart" describes whatever spirit is dominating the person from within the soul, then to describe a person's heart as **"right with God"** indicates a situation where the Holy Spirit is on the throne of the soul and exercising the will of God through the human spirit's obedience, and together they dominate the soul and the life of that person for God. However, if, for example, a **spirit of greed** dominates the life of a person, they can be described as having a heart full of greed (spiritually, not physically).

(ii) Warnings.

(a) Beware the Counterfeit.

What the deliverance minister "picks up" in his spirit from within the person with whom he has contact, is given to him (or her) by the Holy Spirit and this spiritual activity is recorded in the scriptures as the gift of discerning of spirits (1 Cor. 12:10). However, beware of the counterfeit gift of satan whereby witches and other occultists can discern, not only the Holy Spirit in you, but also any unclean spirit still residing in your soul. Non-christians who are spiritually sensitive can often shock the Christian by being more perceptive than they are, but the non-christians' gift is not from God but from the kingdom of the enemy.

Let us therefore establish a very important observation — that **every spiritually aware person is not necessarily operating in the power of the Holy Spirit.** Just as the Holy Spirit in a Christian will pick up problems in other people and witness about them to your human spirit, so also the problem spirits in others will be alarmed at the Holy Spirit in you, and they may take an instinctive, instant dislike to you (or alternatively be drawn to you if they know they need help) without consciously knowing why.

Witches, or any occultists, may be quite sensitive to the condition of the soul of both Christians and non-christians. Indeed, occultists may be more discerning than untrained Christians because of their unclean soul-power. The problem for the Christian pastor is complicated even more when the **spiritually sensitive occultist** is converted to Christ because then, with the Holy Spirit coming into the soul to dwell[1] in the midst of all the remaining unclean spirits, the person's spiritual sensitivity is now inspired by TWO sources, **the Holy and the unclean**, so that they themselves cannot tell the difference until they mature further in Christ.

However there is at least one very good indicator that a person is getting their discernment from the powers of darkness, and that is the fear (and sometimes even terror) generated by the discernment. Someone may come rushing up to you and say, "I don't sit near Jack Spratt in church, because when I do, he always tries to **put something on me!**" — meaning, of course, that what is **in** Jack Spratt seeks to link up with, control and/or harm them.

Someone else might say "Mary Brown has got strong spirits and she is trying to **plug into me.**" The phrasing may be different but the notion is one of plugging into, sending a shaft into, clawing at or putting something spiritually unclean onto or into someone else for the purposes of harming them. The people who

1 See Chap. 1 (vi) (a)

discern in this way are always genuinely troubled and need help, and cannot understand why others (especially ministers) do not see what they can see. They believe their discernment is from the Lord and so they beseech their minister to minister to them accordingly.

Such discernment is always based on fear and serves the purposes of fear, and therefore is almost certainly inspired by occult spirits, not the Holy Spirit. When the Holy Spirit gives discernment He does so for the purposes of comfort and consolation, for the equipping and strengthening of His people (cf. the gift of prophecy — 1 Cor. 14:3), so that victory can be taken in the Name of the lord Jesus Christ.

What does the minister do? Should he or she minister according to discernment given from an unclean source? Generally speaking — NO! You cannot afford to have your ministry come under the control of unclean spirits, no matter how "accurate" they may appear to be. Your ministry must ALWAYS be led by the Holy Spirit. On the other hand, IF the Holy Spirit in you witnesses that the discernment has come from the HOLY Spirit in the sufferer, then that is a different matter — you have His leading to minister accordingly.

This mixture of kingdoms in the hearts of Christians is a problem of enormous magnitude within the Body of Christ, and is responsible for Christians giving false teaching, prophecies, advice and counselling, etc. and **it will be with us until the Bride has truly made herself ready for the Bridegroom.** The level of discernment and perception which is necessary for self-purification is what the apostle Paul meant when he wrote:

> " ... it is my prayer that your love may abound yet more and more **in full knowledge and all perception, that you may test (examine) the things that differ,** in order that you may be pure and blameless in the Day of Christ ..."
>
> Philip. 1:9–10

We badly need this prayer to be prayed and answered today.

What we must do in the immediate future, beginning NOW, is to learn by the Holy Spirit to DISCERN and make the right distinctions, and then set about casting out the deception. While we should be aware of this counterfeit gift and the magnitude of its influence, we are more concerned in this section to direct our attention to the operation of the gift of the Spirit of Jesus Christ by which we discern spirits in any and every kind of situation.

(b) Beware Enemy Agents

Let us say right now that if your church adds deliverance to its spiritual weaponry, it will know both the blessing of God and the counter-activity of the evil one. This counter-activity will certainly include the attempt to **infiltrate your church or your deliverance groups** with demons commissioned to **disrupt, exhaust, discourage** and **disintegrate** the work the Lord has given you to do for Him. You will already have people in your church with spiritual agencies within them which satan will marshal against the work, and he will try to add "specialists" to these, so it becomes vital at the outset to sift, discern, and **to speak lovingly but plainly** with those enquiring to receive ministry. Having said that, it should be stressed that no case is too hard for the Lord, and many times we have seen people sent for the purposes of disruption and destruction (unbeknown to themselves), cleansed from the very agencies that satan hoped to use against the work. However, this can only be done (humanly speaking) where **the sufferer's spirit wants to be free and cooperates with the requirements of the ministry**. Discernment will probably operate progressively throughout the ministry to the sufferer. The Lord seems to give enough discernment to get the ministry started and, as the "trouble spots" are cleansed, so then He reveals the next area of battle. It is far better to let Him direct your operations in this manner rather than to proceed by your own logic. When He gives a Word of Knowledge direct from the Spirit, give it top priority.

(c) Beware Pride.

It is also **not** always advisable to pass on what you have discerned to others who are going to minister deliverance without your involvement. The Lord gives discernment that you might go into battle and win, and **He gives the power to go with the discernment.** You may be able to pass on your discernment to another minister but **you cannot pass on the power**, the anointing of God that empowers your ministry. If you have been given the discernment, then you should minister against the thing discerned, or at least be available, close at hand, in case you are needed. In any event, discernment calls for the exercise of Godly direction and wisdom, that it might bring a blessing to the Church of God for the glory of God, rather than cause unnecessary stumbling, and glory to the discerner. Remember that the giver of discernment is God and He never does anything without a reason. If He entrusts you with spiritual discernment, it is for His own high purposes and glory — not yours. Godly discretion is essential — ask yourself why has God revealed something to you and what does He want you to do — if anything. Many times it will be just as a warning — that you might know the enemy agent that can be used against you (or others) and thus be on your (spiritual) guard. There are normally three reasons why the Lord gives discernment or knowledge, that you may:

1)   be trained for future warfare

2)   be warned against imminent enemy attacks

3)   enter into battle and overcome, now — or soon.

(iii) How to Develop Discernment.

This is a supernatural gift and you are either given it by the Spirit or you are not, but like any gift from God, **it can be asked**

for and increased by practice and experience. Discernment is not something one can classically turn on and off (like preaching or tongues) but it can happen in the most unexpected places and times. It is a gift developed in you by the Spirit Himself, although obviously the more one endeavours to be sensitive to Him and expose oneself to deliverance and counseling situations, the more opportunities there are for the Holy Spirit to teach the minister and operate through him. One can "help" in one's own training by endeavouring to tune-in spiritually to the soul of the sufferer, getting behind the flesh or the face and sensing the spirit operating behind the mask (cf. Heb. 5:13–14).

There may be many ways to develop this gift, but let me tell you one way. Back in 1970 when I was into healing and just touching on the deliverance ministry, I was very impressed with the ministry of Pastor Roger Waters, and particularly with his ability to discern. Later I was able to talk with him and asked him how he received the gift and how it operated. He shared with me the concept that when two Christians meet for any Christian purpose, Christ is in their midst. When a Christian counsellor interviews a sufferer, Christ is there with them both. The sufferer tells his or her problem — spells it out — and so the problem is there between the two of them, and Christ the Answer is also there between the two of them. Christ knows the real problems far better than the sufferer does and He knows the way to win any ensuing battle. **What the counselor has to do is to tune in spiritually to what the sufferer is saying, and even more importantly, to what the Spirit of Christ is saying**. It is a case of listening to what the Spirit is saying in any given situation. Armed with this piece of advice from Roger, I was somewhat prepared when deliverance "caught on" at my church. I would sit down with people and they would open up about their problems. Because of the film "**The Exorcist**" being screened at the time, the numbers grew so rapidly I was forced to make notes of key areas needing ministry. Thus to begin it was somewhat a scientific method, using the mind

AND the Spirit. People would spell out their problems such as alcohol or smoking, and it was easy to deduce that strong drink and nicotine spirits were inspiring the slavery of the sufferer. You don't have to be gifted to work out those problems. If a lad was disruptive in class and destroyed teaching situations at school, it was a simple matter to see the effects caused by a spirit in order to name it. If the effect is destruction, then the cause can safely be labelled a spirit of destruction. Simple; logical — **we look at the effect in order to name the cause**, and using this principle helped a great deal when faced with problems a little less obvious.

After taking personal and confidential history sheets on a few dozen sufferers, one begins to notice the **physical appearance** of the sufferers, particularly the **eyes**, the **clothing**, the **voice**, the **jewelery**, the **skin**, the **mouth**. For example, even non-christians can "pick up" or sense a spirit of homosexuality by appearance at times, and it can be just as simple to discern fear and terror, witchcraft and destruction. One begins to learn by observance that certain groupings of spirits in a kingdom in the human soul are common. Homosexual spirits are invariably linked with destruction and confusion; epilepsy and unbelief with spiritism. With experience one begins to pick up in the spirit the look in the eyes that tells of lust, anger, hatred, arrogance, smugness, deception and snobbery; the **shape** of a person may reveal a gluttony problem and **what they wear** may reveal a level of vanity, attention-getting and glory-seeking. What sort of spirits would you think inspire the martial arts? Yes, you are right — destruction, religious and mind-binding or mind-control spirits — these latter being very, very common in **all non-christian, religious and heretical** movements, areas of **political fanaticism, radicalism** and **hypnosis.**

Our sense of (spiritual) **smell** is also very helpful. I don't have to remind you that unclean spirits smell unclean and can cause halitosis and body odor, etc.

An unusual testimony to the validity of discernment by smell springs to mind here. It is notable for the fact that it concerns two mature Christians whose commitment to the Lord and mature judgment I respect. On separate occasions these Christians warned me about the dangers of someone else's ministry. "Be careful", they said, "that ministry is way out and not of the Lord!" I thought otherwise, but because I respected these people so much I began to doubt. Maybe they were right? Maybe so-and-so's ministry WAS counterfeit and I had better withdraw my support?

However, on each occasion, just as the seeds of doubt began to be received into my heart, the good Lord gave me a whif of my companion's breath. **On each occasion it stank**, and I instantly realised that my companion was speaking under the inspiration of an unclean spirit. I praise the Lord for His grace and revelation to me.

This happened with two different people on two separate occasions concerning the same ministry. They meant well. They thought they had the mind of Christ. It was just that the Lord was moving in a way that their tiny minds could not comprehend, and He "failed" to consult them first! (Romans 11:33–34).

Very soon you will find that discernment by questioning and obtaining answers is being substantially assisted by discernment purely by the Spirit through receiving a Word of knowledge. This gift can progress to the point that, not only are you given the character of a certain spirit but also its NAME and exactly where it is located in the sufferer's body. When I worked in a Full Salvation Ministry many years ago, the Director would minister deliverance to a group of nearly one hundred people, and she knew what was troubling each one and where the trouble spot was in each body. How? Because she also suffered (in the spirit) the same problem in her own body. This is highly developed discernment and enables the minister to work most effectively. How can this be explained theologically? Perhaps it is because Christ bore our

sicknesses (Matt.8:16–17), our **griefs, pains** and **sorrows** (Isaiah 53:4–5), during His agony, passion and crucifixion, and by His **bruise** we have been healed (Gen. 3:15, Isa. 53:5,10, 1 Peter 2:24). Thus we who are crucified with Christ and have put to death the flesh no longer live but Christ lives in us (Gal. 2:20). Therefore His sickness-bearing on the Cross is something with which the Word of God associates us. **If our crucifixion identifies us with Jesus' crucifixion**, then the crucified Christ within us may enable us to experience otherwise unsearchable things.[1] Who is sufficient for these things? (2 Cor. 2:16).

Finally there is revelational discernment. Recently I watched a **daytime television host** have a bit of a giggle on the question of death, and life after death with a panel of guests and before a studio audience. These serious matters were treated in a mocking, humorous manner and, after the host had made a joke in unfortunate taste, we were shown a view of the studio audience laughing. In that split moment of time the Holy Spirit revealed to me, not elderly, jolly matrons enjoying a joke, but rows of ugly little demons in dwarf bodies mocking the promises of God.

(iv) Summary

Let us now recapitulate in brief the various methods of discerning of spirits (known to me) that are available to us from the Lord:

1) The "Personal Particulars" Sheet

We record in this confidential form the personal details that the sufferer tells us about their occult, medical and personality background during counselling. This form will be described in more detail in the next chapter.

---

1 See "The Stigmata of Jesus" for a full scriptural exposition.

2) Observation of external evidence

External evidence shows forth a portion of the hidden heart just as an iceberg protruding above the ocean warns of hidden dangers. Clothing, skin, conversation (both words and tonal sounds), eyes, mouth and expression af the total face, not to forget smell, posture and shape.

3) Experience of groupings (kingdoms)

Kingdoms of darkness in the human soul are made up of groupings of various spirits, and one can exercise an accurate discernment simply by knowing from experience that certain obvious spirits usually have an association with others "worse than themselves". For example, **unbelief** or **epilepsy** immediately suggest **spiritism**, and **homosexuality** ALWAYS keeps company with **destruction** and **confusion**. **Confusion** spirits are always the tip of the iceberg of "**mind-control**" or "**mind-binding**" rulers. Once we have those, we are awake to the possibility of **brain damage** caused by drugs and their base of **witchcraft** and **destruction**. Only experience can teach you this (Heb. 5:13–14). It is the Lord's doing and marvelous in our eyes (Ps. 118:23).

4) A Word of Knowledge

How can we liken the gift of a **Word of Knowledge** with the gift of **discerning of spirits**? Perhaps we can better see the relationship between the two if we first compare the relationship between **miracles** and **healings**. Fast healings are miracles, of course, but not every miracle is a healing. Healing miracles are a special form of miracle, and miracles that are not healings are simply (other) miracles. For example, feeding the 5000 plus people by Jesus was a

miracle of provision, not healing. Likewise with knowledge and discernment. Clearly when the Holy Spirit reveals a spirit of fear to you, that is discernment because you have discerned a spirit. All discernment is knowledge, but not all knowledge is discerning of spirits. During an interview with a young man I was given a Word of Knowledge, "boxing". It turned out that his father had been a boxer and hereditary problems were involved; so the Holy Spirit had given the key background to a whole set of problems and spirits.

Some while ago Verlie made me laugh when I saw her bend down and rebuke the spirit of **vituperation** in someone's ear. I thought "That's a big word, where did she get that from?" — knowing full well the answer.

The laugh came after the meeting when I found her thumbing through the Concise Oxford Dictionary at home. She explained she was looking up "vituperation" to see what it meant.

"How could you call out a spirit when you don't know the meaning of its name?" I asked. "That's what the Holy Spirit gave me. I don't have to know what it means", she replied. This is no longer a rare occurrence and when I see Verlie picking up the Dictionary I know what is coming and we have a little smile together when we realize that the Lord is not limited by our limited vocabulary. This, of course, is a beautiful confirmation from the Lord that she is not operating in the flesh, but in the Spirit.

So then, a direct Word of Knowledge may be given by the Lord to open up a whole range of discernment, pin-pointing the place to commence the ministry. The Lord knows the weakest part of the enemy's defenses and if we let Him run the battle, the enemy will begin to crumple (e.g. Jericho). It is not wrong to check with the Lord to get a double or triple confirmation (second or third witness) if you are in doubt about the Word given. The Lord is gracious with His children, and patient in teaching us.

5) **Intercessory Suffering (empathy)**

Being crucified with Christ is the legal position and experience of every true Christian (Rom. 6:6), but of course some of us have been more successful than others in putting to death the things of the flesh. Because we have shared in the crucifixion of Jesus, and Jesus bore our sickness and pains, we too may experience the sickness-bearing of Christ on behalf of the sufferer IN OUR OWN BODIES! A person gifted in this way experiences and shares in the suffering of the sufferer, knowing exactly where the problem is located, and knowing also that, because one is experiencing the sickness-bearing of Christ, healing and/or deliverance is certain, **if the subject can receive it.**

6) **"Revelational" discernment**

By this we mean the discerning of spirits by spiritual revelation or vision, where we are permitted to see into the spiritual realm with our spiritual eyes and actually see the enemy spirits in all their ugliness. Up to the time of writing, this kind of discernment does not seem to have been very common; perhaps because it is a privilege, a special grace, rather than a necessity for the Body of Christ. The enemy is not a pretty sight. It is bad enough having to see them when they are hidden behind the eyes, the mouths and the expressions of human beings, without having to see them apart from their "cover".

Most discernment is a combination of several of these methods. We have isolated and discussed each method purely for the purposes of teaching and study, but in practice they overlap and complement each other, giving you the step by step corroboration and witness of the Holy Spirit desirable before proceeding. Sometimes we are not even aware of the processes. All we know is that we have spiritual information about a person and we do not immediately know how we know. When we stop and think about it later, we may be able to discover the method the Holy Spirit used, and maybe we won't. Sometimes there is just a "knowing in the Spirit" which one could easily call a Word of Knowledge.

Beware of the counterfeits of these gifts. By their fruits you shall know them.

When we begin to exercise the gift of discerning of spirits we can be likened to a soldier with a machine-gun. We may spray a lot of bullets about and hit very little. As we learn from experience, we hit more and more of the enemy. There is less waste of bullets and more success. We may become so good, so accurate, that our officer selects us for sniper training. We are now so accurate that it only needs one bullet for one enemy soldier.

Likewise in the Lord's army. We may command twenty different kinds of spirit out of a sufferer and "hit" only two or three in the beginning. That is not wrong. We each have to begin somewhere, and better to count the hits rather than the misses. However as the Lord sharpens our spiritual skill I believe there will be less wasteage and more victories until we are more like an experienced spiritual sniper.

One bullet — one enemy — no waste!
(name)   (spirit)   (guess-work)

I don't pretend to know all about this subject[1] — who does? But what I have shared is a beginning. Now it is between you and the Lord, for it is a gift (a charisma) from Him.

---

1 Further information on this subject of discerning of spirits is available in Books 2,3 and 4.

7. Spiritual Hosts of Wickedness.

One of our key scripture texts has been: "**We do not wrestle with blood and flesh but with rulers and authorities...**" and when we stop to think about this and begin to take Paul's words seriously, we find that they strongly infer that the whole struggle of life is a struggle against unclean spirits. Since it is obvious that every day carries its own challenges (indeed Jesus taught us that every day presents us with more than enough evil — Matt. 6:34), we begin to get the impression that we are literally surrounded by the hosts of darkness seeking to trip us up wherever possible. Is this being negative? No, we are only saying what the Bible says, and the Bible is not a negative book — it is the revelation of God's victory over the rulers and authorities through Jesus Christ. Thus Christians who are "in Christ" have nothing to fear — there is no need to hide one's head in the sand rather than look the enemy in the eye. The enormity and complexity of satan's hordes are being revealed by the Holy Spirit today in a way that no generation before us has ever experienced. We have never understood or even scratched the surface of another well-known Bible phrase: "**the whole world lies in (the power of) the evil one**". Would you please read that phrase — slowly — three times — and really let it sink in? If you have done that you will more readily and easily understand the following experiences recording the variety of unclean spirits encountered during deliverance ministry.

(i) **Creation Spirits**. (The *Stoicheia* – Gal. 4:3, 8–9; Col. 2:8, 20; 2 Peter 3:8,10 RSV).

An interesting incident takes place in the book of Acts where a clairvoyant, occult woman had a spirit of divination cast out of her. Literally this should be translated "**the spirit of a python**" (Acts 16:16). I have known many cases where the spirit of a snake (including python), of a tiger, and of various other animals and birds have been manifested. There are people who have monkey faces, gorilla faces, ferret and foxy faces; there are people who remind us of cats, pigs, frogs, various kinds of dogs, sparrows, owls, various birds of prey (hawks, vultures), snakes and reptiles, etc.

One beautiful Christian lady receiving deliverance ministry had a pronounced problem with servility. She was very much under her husband's thumb in an unclean way but, of course, thought she was being submissive in a Godly way and took the bullying as her Christian duty.

Then the Lord revealed **mouse** spirits controlling her and by the grace of God they were removed. To everyone's surprise however, her servility turned to anger and aggression and now a **tiger** spirit emerged from deep within her soul, together with **religious** spirits. This meant that she changed from a person with a "submissive" attitude to an aggressively religious person and needed further ministry for those problems.

It is well to note here that Christians being cleaned out by means of **a regular Deliverance and Restoration program** may sometimes seem to get worse before they get better. But who would have thought (in the natural) that both mouse and tiger spirits could occupy the same soul?

In fact the whole area of INVISIBLE creation is one where we have only scanty information from the Word of God but nevertheless it probably has more to tell us than we first realised. As well as the revelation of the existence of the spirit of a python inspiring a fortune-teller the following scriptures are worth a second look.

> The LORD says to Israel: "I will restore to you the years that the **locust** has eaten, the **cankerworm** and the **caterpillar** and the **palmerworm**, my great army which I sent among, you."
>
> Joel 2:25

The question is — are these insects a literal and physical army or is the Lord talking about a SPIRITUAL, UNSEEN army? There appears to be no similar prior reference to such insects in the Bible but earlier in the same chapter it seems they make their appearance at the Day of the Lord, that is, about Judgment time. Also the New Testament has an interesting revelation on **locusts** (Rev. 9:7–11) which supports the view that the army is spiritual. We are not denying the physical, but simply emphasizing the spiritual. Obviously both physical AND spiritual interpretations are necessary for many passages in the Bible.

The Bible also talks of a spiritual **hornet** which won victory for Israel in the Promised Land:

> "And I sent the HORNET before you, which drove them out from before you, the two kings of the Amorites; not with your swords or your bow."
>
> Josh. 24:12

In the battles that Israel fought for the Promised Land **there is no reference to an army or swarm of physical hornets** descending upon the Amorites in order to give Israel victory, but here the Lord plainly says that they did not win the battle by their own physical weapons but by His intervention, probably supernatural and invisible. The earthly battle was fought with sword and bow, but it was won in the heavenlies, in the spiritual realm, by **God's hornet**.

Similarly the tramping of the Israelites out of Egypt and through the wilderness to Mount Sinai with all its dangers and drama may have been made on foot, physically, but they survived because **in the spiritual, invisible realm they were borne on eagles wings** (Exod. 19:4).

According to one of King David's prophetic psalms, when Jesus hung on the Cross and looked down on the crowd mocking, reviling and abusing Him, He did not see people, but **animal spirits manifesting THROUGH people** — their teeth bared, nostrils flaring and their lips curled back as they hurled abuse at the Lamb of God. "If you be the Son of God come down from the Cross!" and "He saved others let Him save Himself!" Psalm 22 tells us that Jesus saw **bulls** and **dogs** surrounding Him.

> "Many **bulls** have compassed me
> Strong **bulls** of Bashan have beset me round
> They gape upon me with their mouth
> As a ravening and roaring lion".
>
> Ps. 22:12–13

> "For **dogs** have compassed me
> The assembly of evil-doers have enclosed me
> They pierced my hands and my feet" (v. 16).

Plainly the Lord Jesus was not seeing flesh and blood but was looking into the SPIRITUAL natures of those surrounding Him, perceiving the attack of the unclean SPIRIT world THROUGH bulls (Jews?) and dogs (Gentiles?).

We hardly need to add that the **self-righteous, traditional, religious Pharisees** are seen in the spiritual realm of things as **vipers** (Matt. 3:7, 23:27–33), that the harlot church (as distinct from the true Church — the Bride of Christ) is the home of every unclean spirit and every unclean hateful **bird** (spirit) (Rev. 18:2).

There is yet another hint of the spiritual nature of things operating invisibly behind the physical elements we normally see in the incident of Jesus stilling the storm on the Sea of Galilee. He commanded the wind and the sea, literally, "Be silent, BE MUZZLED!" He spoke to the elements as if they were some **huge invisible animal or beast** that was snarling and gnashing its teeth at the disciples in the boat and needed MUZZLING! (Mark 4:39). Taking this a step further, and it is a big step, perhaps we have erred in interpreting **the beasts in the book of Revelation** as being metaphorical or pictorial beasts but not real beings. They could well be spiritual beings, like satan himself. It is only our tiny minds and lack of information about the spiritual world — demonic and Godly — which encourages us to settle for lesser but more acceptable explanations of prophecy (see Rev. 13:1–4, 11–15, cf. 12:9, 12–17).

Let us re-think yet another scripture. **Mr Peter Horrobin**, Director of Ellel Ministries, near Lancaster, England, believes that the **wild beasts** referred to in Ezekiel's condemnation of false and slack shepherds have a very real meaning for today, because they are in fact demonic, invisible, **spiritual** beasts that we fight against, now, in the New Testament age, and not simply a parable applicable only to Ezekiel's time (Ezek. 34:5, 8, 25, 28). In view of the evidence we have just considered how can any serious Bible student disagree with him?

Many Christians sense in their spirit that they are waging war against spiritual animals or beasts, and are therefore attracted to a form of prayer seeking the Lord's daily protection. While some Christians pray for the sprinkling of the blood (Heb. 12:24, 1 Pet. 1:2) of the Passover Lamb (1 Cor. 5:7) for daily protection — **others ask for the Lord to put a hedge about them** (Job 1:10). What is a hedge for? — It is to keep the wild beasts at bay. Then why do Christians ask for this, since there are no wild beasts to threaten us in Washington (U.S.A.) or London (U.K.) or Sydney (Australia)?

Surely the implication is to keep SPIRITUAL beasts at bay? **Prayer is spiritual, the hedge is spiritual and the enemy is spiritual**. Christians who pray in this way are simply acknowledging the reality of spiritual beasts amongst our enemies.

Apparently there is no limit to the parallels that are possible from the realm of the flesh to the realm of the spiritual world. Hard to believe? Then ponder again 'the spirit of a python' and ask yourself what is the Word of God saying to us with this revealing phrase.

Consider the case where a Christian missionary in India told a visiting evangelist that he could tell which god various people worshipped by the way they walked, and illustrated his point by Indicating people who worshipped an **elephant** god as these people lumbered by. Like any other unclean spirit, creation spirits stamp their character upon the person they inhabit and this is often observable, even to those without much discernment.

The more people impress us in this way, the more aware we need to be regarding the imagery which they have taken on from satan (Rom. 1:23–25) instead of the imagery of Jesus, the Son of God (Rom. 8:29), who is also man made in the image of God (2 Cor. 4:4). A factor that disturbs me greatly (although it is not at all surprising when we understand who rules the world) is the increase of **films depicting animals or monsters** (usually quite hideous) in abnormally close fellowship with human beings. This theme seemed to really get under way with the film "Planet of the Apes", and since then hideous things with appearances designed to horrify have been presented as poor, gentle, good, misunderstood friends of mankind. I sense that viewers are being programmed and softened up for an invasion of animal spirits, if they are not already affected; or at the very least, our children are being prepared by the evil genius of the destroyer, satan, to accept, communicate and be friendly with every hideous, foul and corrupting thing in his ugly kingdom (compare the film "E.T."?).

Please remember that we are not talking about flesh; we are talking about spirit — the spirit that rules and stamps its character and image upon the flesh (Eph.2:2).

The interest in animals and all living things in creation by children is probably a development from their love of a pet in their backyard, graduating to monsters on the television screen. To underline this soulish interest in the very young, we should note that it is customary even in Christian societies to give dolls to little girls and **teddy bears** to little boys. One might attempt to justify giving dolls to little girls on the grounds of satisfying their basic motherhood instincts, so that they can copy their mother and lavish love, care and affection (and perhaps practice a little domination) on a "baby" which, when you think about it, is really the image or idol of a baby, but how do we attempt to justify **teddy bears** for little boys?

When we stop to think about it we realize such a practice is really quite illogical or irrational. It is difficult to see any training for the future in this at all. One might argue that some little boys would be just as happy with a model puppy (dog), but if that is the case WHY do we give BEARS? The answer is partly that BEARS SATISFY the SOULISH and mysterious LONGING for the little one for a relationship of love **and protection**, which may take years to disappear.

I remember well enough to know that I lavished love (and sometimes a little "cruelty") on my own teddy and also at times found great security and comfort in having him in bed with me. **What strange creatures we are** when even as little children, we can IDENTIFY with, and believe we are protected by, speechless, inanimate objects which can never repay the trust we place in them (cf. Jeremiah 10:3–5).

When we grow up, of course, **our relationship with creation spirits can be quite sinister**, e.g. **a prostitute** who received deliverance from unclean spirits drew me pictures of **weird, furry animal shapes** of the spirits that were tormenting her. **Gary Gilmore,** the American mass murderer who insisted on being executed at the end of 1976 and succeeded in January, 1977 drew pictures of the **various animal spirits** that were tormenting him in prison, and they were published in the American press.

Gilmore wrote to his girl-friend from prison in September, 1976 as follows:

"I've told you that I haven't slept. The ghosts have descended and set upon me with a force I didn't believe they possessed."

"They're slippery, sneaky and get tangled in your hair like bats ... **demons with dirty, furry bodies** whispering vile things, chortling and laughing with a hideous glee to see me toss sleepless".

"They plan to pounce upon me in a shrieking, mad fury when I leave (this life), with their hideous long toe and finger claws and teeth dripping with rank saliva ... **dirty inhuman beasts,** creeping, crawling, red-eyed, soulless beasts".

'They bite and claw, scratch and screech. They beckon with crooked finger. They call: 'You have to come one day. Come now, Gary, you murderous fiend'. Their aim is to recruit me. And their method is to destroy hope, then reason. They won't let me have a night's sleep. I smack them down, but they sneak back and climb in my ears and tell me foul jokes. They want to sap my strength, drain my hope ... leave me derelict, lost, alone. I just endure and counterpunch when I can. I need a silver sword against them".

"They beset me, but I will shake them yet. I will slay and scatter them with the silver sword of love. You are my Nicole. Love me — give me the silver sword. They will never recruit me. They might attack me, but they will never prevail ... never in all their shrieking, screeching insanity".

In the same letter, Gilmore refers to another time the ghosts attacked him years ago. He was chained to a bed in solitary confinement while serving time for robbery at an Oregon prison.

"They jumped on me like fiends when I was chained to that bed. They laughed with glee and **made a circle with joined paws and long, three fingered hands**. They thought they had me. I endured a constant onslaught of demon fury".

"It left me drained and fifty pounds lighter. They like it when I hurt. And I have been burning lately. I hate to say it, but in the last week they almost got me. They came the closest that they ever have".

(National Enquirer, 18/1/77)

Doreen Irvine in her life-story[1] wrote:

"I experienced the most horrific dreams ... **Ugly hairy animals** chased me to a dark bottomless pit, hands clawed at my body, my throat. Marks were evident on my body when I awoke."

It is highly possible that **vampire legends** are, in reality, based on the activity of **animal spirits**. The truth of the matter is that **creation spirits** — what the scriptures call **the beggarly and elemental spirits of the universe** (Col. 2:8, 20) — are rife throughout all forms of societies and cultures, INCLUDING CHRISTIAN. It surprises us today that they are there because they have never been exposed before, but they are coming out into the open more and more in these last days, and we are going to be absolutely amazed at the extent of their activities. In other words, the incident of Paul casting out the **spirit of a python** is not recorded in Holy Scripture so that we Christians might view it as an isolated or rare conflict which we can pass over quickly (by translating "python" as "divination"), but **it is recorded for our benefit TODAY as a KEY deliverance**, because it opens up

---

1 "From Witchcraft to Christ", p.135. See also "Bitten by Devils" by Lester Sumrall.

our understanding to a widespread area of satanic activity and human need, together with the Lord's powerful solution.

In our ministry experience we have found various **snake** and serpent spirits very, very common, and only recently my wife, Verlie, received a Word of Knowledge to concentrate on "**wolf**" spirits during a deliverance meeting. There were several manifestations and the results very pleasing.

Tiger spirits are common where the human problem concerns murder and blood-lust, and where violent sports are exercised, such as boxing, and even quite common in the ladies. Very common in people who experience RAGE, whether controlled or uncontrolled.

Manifestations of **animal spirits** in people are also observable from their **attitude to animals**, and the clothes they wear. Nobody seems to know why women dressing in **leopard-skin** swimsuits, pants suits, play suits and dresses are considered as a sexual "turn-on" for males as well as a female "come-on;" likewise with (shiny) leather jackets, slacks and boots, and also animal fur clothes. Apparently there is an area of unclean "kinky" sexual behaviour where animal furs, skins and other paraphernalia are used. Why is this so?

LUST IS ANIMALISTIC

The answer is very simple. Animal spirits and lust spirits combine to draw together and link with each other in what is often thought of as "the right chemistry" or "animal magnetism" (well put) or "sensuality" (feline variety) or "passion". **Such attraction is sought after and applauded by the world, but its source is utterly unclean and hostile to God's will and God's Word**; hence we are told to "flee from youthful lusts and follow after righteousness" (2 Tim. 2:22), and "to abstain from the passions of the flesh that WAGE WAR AGAINST YOUR SOUL" (1 Peter 2:11). Rapists are often described as animals, beasts and monsters, and this may be closer to the **spiritual** truth than many realize.

Animal spirits which draw human beings into unclean sexual behavior tend to lead their victims to degenerate from one degree of "kinkiness" into even greater degrees of depravity such as **bestiality**, where animal spirits actually use human beings in order to fornicate with physical animals. However, when we identify **animal** spirits, we mean that to include **reptile** spirits and other creation spirits as well, such as **birds** and **insects**. **Praise the Lord that human beings can be set free from all this garbage in Jesus' Name!**

A woman of my acquaintance, who was suffering from intense pain to the point of losing consciousness, saw in the spirit **scorpion**-like creatures crawling across the ceiling. When she rebuked them in Jesus' Name they scurried away to the corners of the room; then proceeded to advance on her again until the rebuke was repeated. She blesses God for bringing her through that time of testing, and healing her.

After this, maybe drunks who see **pink elephants** have a point to consider. There are two possible explanations regarding hallucinations "seen" by alcoholics or other drug-affected people. Either they really do see the "things" they are talking to, or they don't. We know from the occult practice of hypnosis that, in the hands of a trained hypnotist, a subject may be deceived into believing that the **old brown shoe** that they are stroking on their lap is really a **lovely, warm, friendly puppy-dog**. **The natural sense of "seeing" is set aside and a deceptive illusion (delusion!) created by hypnotic suggestion produces a lie**. Perhaps "hallucinations" are in that category, OR perhaps the unclean spirit in the drug-taker, using human eyes, sees into the spirit world and actually enables a human to see real spiritual beings or animals normally invisible to our natural sight. Only recently, Verlie was nursing a lady who, **suffering from withdrawal symptoms**, "saw" a nice home with two dogs on a sofa, barking. Other people talk vigorously to invisible company around them. This is observable in the streets of any area known to be frequented by **alcoholics**. The question is, are they victims of an illusion of their damaged minds, or do they see things in the spirit that are really there? If you believe the former, you then have the problem of who or what (in the absence of a human source of suggestion, e.g. hypnotist) is the source creator of the illusion. If we agree that every effect must have a cause, and if we have acknowledged the reality of the spiritual realm (and entered into it by receiving the Spirit of Jesus ourselves), we come back to two possibilities. Either (i) people see true spiritual beings in the spiritual world or (ii) people are affected by the activity of a spirit of distortion or deception creating illusions. **Whichever way we look at it, the answer is not fleshly but spiritual**. If you are going to be satisfied with a flesh answer alone (e.g. brain damage), then you may make a "good" Doctor but not such a good Pastor. You may give help to the flesh but not the soul.

(ii) Racist or Religious?

We begin to take on the image of the spirit that controls us. Contrary to popular opinion, **racial or national facial features** do not reflect the *climate* of a native country but rather the **religious spirit** ruling a human life. Inhabitants of Asia are dominated by various eastern religions and their facial appearances reflect centuries of idol worship. Most people think there are German faces, English faces, African faces, Asian faces etc., **but put Jesus Christ into their hearts and they all begin to have Jesus faces.**

Turks generally have a very **Muslim** look about them. It is not that they look Turkish (a nationalistic thing) but they look Islamic (a spiritual thing). We have been deceived into thinking that today's problems of communication in the world are basically racist or political, ideological and philosophical when in fact **they touch the spirit and soul of men — they are spiritual.** The conflict is **spiritual** — between Christ and antichrist.

So it is not being racist but simply truthful in revealing the driving soul force of Islam in the personality. A case in point — observe your **western men** who adopt **an eastern transcendental meditational religion**. Do they retain their outward western image or do they appear to make some kind of transition into the spirit of the religion of their adoption? Observe those who advance in their new-found religion — look for piercing snake-like eyes that glitter, particularly when annoyed, and use your gift of discerning of spirits.

(iii) Infirmity Spirits.

Under the general heading of infirmity, one could name just about every sickness and disease in the medical books, and even those that aren't. Remember, the key is that **every physical corruption ultimately has a spiritual cause**. It is the old law of cause and effect where the cause is spiritual and invisible and the effect is physical and visible — even if only under a microscope. Some infirmities lend themselves more easily to the notion of being **psychosomatic**, but it is interesting to notice that more and more doctors are viewing sickness as psychosomatic in origin.

This awareness was highlighted in March 1988 by conferences held in Canberra and Sydney entitled "Health and Medicine of the Future". Michael Cameron reported in the Daily Mirror:

> Feeling crook today? Well blame it on a long-dead enemy of great-auntie Agatha who could be "haunting" you with illness.
>
> Amazing new research claims that many of our health problems are caused by **curses** put on us by ghosts.
>
> The spooks put spanners in our bodyworks, say physicians, as a way of getting their own back for wrongs done to them in their own lives.

The spirits — those of ancestors or people who hated them — could be to blame for as much as **80 per cent of all our illnesses**, according to a group which presents its findings at the weekend.

A dozen international researchers meet in Canberra tomorrow and in Sydney on Sunday to address a conference called Health and Medicine of the Future.

Among the claims they will put forward are that spirits can cause diseases ranging from terminal cancer to mental problems such as manic depression.

Dr Andris Tebecis, a neurosurgeon from Canberra, said:

"There is now good scientific evidence that entities attached to people's bodies cause a vast range of problems with both the body and mind."

Sydney Hospital **gastroenterologist Kowit Bhanthumnavin**, who will also be speaking, said: "Medical Science has failed to solve the world's health problems.

"We are simply saying there could be a new solution." Another researcher, **Professor Zensaku Yoshizawa** of Japan, said: "**After 30 years I am now astonished by the fact that the cause of many fatal diseases, which are beyond medical Science, lies in the spiritual dimension**."

Many alternative medical practitioners are part of the New Age movement and are therefore themselves deceived, but notwithstanding this danger it is clear that many medical scientists acknowledge that physical sickness is often mind (soul) induced, and some even recognise that the causes are spiritual.

"**Psych**" means soul/mind and "**soma**" means body, so "**psychosomatic**" is just another way of saying that many bodily infirmities originate in the soul/mind rather than in body tissues, and with this we can strongly agree.

One thing to beware of is the reaction within many sufferers when **spirits of infirmity** are commanded to leave them.

"**Infirmity**" is a broad word covering every human flaw in body (flesh, bones), mind and soul (emotions). It literally means weakness, frailty or sickness in any part of a living creature and you will remember that a spirit of infirmity had to be cast out of the daughter of Abraham before her deformed spine could be healed (Luke 13:10–13).

However, after a group deliverance meeting in which infirmity spirits have been called out, you can be sure that many people will begin to experience symptoms of **influenza** or **the common cold.** This is to be expected in western nations where flu viruses are caught, locked into the circulatory system and stored away in the body.

Nobody ever gets healed of influenza through medicine; the human body simply overcomes the symptoms and the disease gets stored away, to be brought out again by the enemy (next year?) when conditions (winter?) are favorable again. That is why Doctors can often tell you what is wrong with you (physically) after giving you a blood test. We carry so much infirmity in our blood.

So what happens when you command "Infirmity, loose them in Jesus' Name!"?

Very simply some of them will ring you up during the week and say "Oh Peder, sorry I can't make der meeding on Sunday. I've godda code in der dose (cold in the nose!)."

Until you teach them otherwise, very few will realise they have NOT caught a new cold,[1] but are beginning to get rid of the influenza empire stored in their bodies. If they give in to the symptoms and stay away from your deliverance and healing meeting they lose the battle.

If they can accept your explanation that they are not sick but getting rid of all their stored up infirmity, and follow up by attending your meetings, they will win not only the battle, but the war.

Asthma, of course, is recognised as being psychosomatic in many cases — and we would expect that to be a spirit. **Bronchitis** is very often psychosomatic and so is migraine, and we have seen plenty of those come out and folk set free. **Nightmares**[2], of course, are nasty spirits. You can imagine what could happen with nightmares ruining your sleep night after night. Ugly pictures, waking up in a sweat, tossing and turning, the mind overactive, black pictures, fear clutching you; all caused by a spirit of nightmare — frightening! But thanks be to God — Christ has defeated them all.

Let me repeat that it is a mistake to believe that this ministry is for the uneducated, or for peasants on the mission field, or the primitive cultures; it is for everyone, every creature created by God who has to battle in this life against the principalities and powers. So it becomes impossible to sustain the view that cases of demonization are rare; rather the evidence supports the view that freedom from demonization is rare. If you want to say the devil led you astray, well that's okay, I'm not going to argue with that. If you want to name the prince of demons — and most evangelical Christians would say, "Oh, satan led me astray" — that is okay too! I am just suggesting **a small change in terminology,** that it is demons who led you astray at the instruction, of course, of the prince of demons. I am not saying that Christians are

1 We will say more about incoming and outgoing "junk", especially in Book 3.

2 Increasing today because of horror videos and films, and child abuse.

demon-possessed, but that they are affected by demons. We all are, and no one born into this world will escape because it is a **fallen world.** The world (creation) has fallen from Grace into sin, corruption and death; **mankind has fallen,** and we even have to deal with **fallen angels** (Rev. 12:9). All visible creation has fallen and is subject to decay and death (Rom. 8:19–23). This enormous spiritual pollution is what we are up against, and **the Bible teaches that we are all infected and affected to some extent.**

Praise God for the solution that we have in the Person and the Spirit of the Lord Jesus Christ!

4

PREPARATION OF THE SUFFERER

1. Initial Contact.

If you are a full-time Christian worker, your first contact with a troubled person seeking deliverance will probably be by **phone**, or at the **front door**, if it is not an actual manifestation of an unclean spirit in one of your **church meetings.** The latter would probably require immediate attention without any preamble or preparation, but certainly there should be counseling and further preparation as soon afterwards as possible. When people make a tentative inquiry, because of the heavy demands of this ministry on TIME, I like to give or send interested people a short pamphlet to read entitled "**So You Think You Need Deliverance**", which helps them think about the issues involved and clears a way through their mental confusion so they can at least decide whether they want an interview or not. If the minister can remove the clouds of fear, confusion, embarrassment and mistrust — usually by the exercise of compassionate concern and Godly wisdom — then he has gone a long way to giving real hope — to lifting the human spirit up out of misery — and perhaps, for the first time, the sufferer can see that Jesus really is the answer to their deepest needs just like the New Testament says. He really cares (because His minister cares) and there is light at the end of the tunnel.

(i) Sorting Out Inquires

Broadly speaking, the four things I want to know from an enquirer unknown to me are:

1) Are you a Christian?

2) If not, why not? For example, is there any reason preventing you from receiving all the blessings of Christ?

3) Are you under pastoral authority with another church and, if so, have you sought your shepherd's help?

4) If you are not under pastoral authority, are you prepared to accept our pastoral authority over you in Christ?

A pamphlet can put these four questions to them so that, if an interview is sought after the pamphlet has been read, there is a much greater likelihood of proceeding with the ministry, and therefore **unprofitable interviews are reduced** to a minimum.

Our suggested pamphlet is attached for your study (see Appendix B), and would serve the purpose of offering a biblical solution to troubled people who don't know what deliverance is all about. It helps clarify their thinking whilst removing fear of the unknown, and encourages them to find out the truth. However, the introductory pamphlet is only an aid and may be dispensed with, as the Spirit leads. Usually enquirers are reasonably sure within themselves what is causing their problems, and it is a relief for them to find someone who does not think their experiences are foolish. It is obvious that a great number of unconverted people (who are being oppressed) are going to be brought into the Kingdom of God because of their need of deliverance, in the same way that the need for healing has led many people to Christ.

If the person is clearly not interested in Christianity but simply wants help in order to get relief so that they can continue sinning, then an interview is just wasting your time; but sometimes you will grant an interview in order to make sure. The principle involved is that you want to spend your time in the way that is most profitable to the sufferers and for the extension of the Kingdom of God in people's lives. **Normally a person must be a member of the Kingdom of God (i.e. a Christian) if they are to receive the blessings of the King (i.e. Christ).** As we have said before, ministering Christ's deliverance to an unbeliever may not help them at all but perhaps the contrary, so it is important to sort out the enquirers that are genuinely interested in God's help from those who are not.

Most cases will come out clear-cut:

(a) **people not interested in God and Christianity** who will not get past reading the pamphlet and will not make further enquiry;

(b) **people** who follow up the pamphlet will either be **in the Kingdom of God, or not far from the Kingdom of God** and can be brought into the Kingdom;

(c) **the borderline cases**, perhaps where a pamphlet may not have been used and you're not sure whether the sufferer just wants any help, or God's help, or doesn't know what they want. In such cases an interview will clear the air, in order to give the sufferer every chance to obtain the blessings of Christ.

(ii) Church Allegiance

In relation to questions 3 and 4, the church allegiance of the enquirer was once very important to me. I always sought, wherever possible, to have the permission and active support of the Pastor of the enquirer before proceeding to minister. It was not a matter of their denomination that concerned me, but simply a desire for other pastors to take advantage of our God-given skills so that their people could be blessed without any sense of possessiveness or sheep-stealing coming into the situation. Ideally we wanted, and still want, to minister to people and send them back to their own assemblies as living proof of the goodness of the Lord. Therefore it was our policy to refer people back to their Pastor to get his permission, at the very least, and his cooperation and active support as well, if possible.

In theory this was all very neat and designed to keep us out of trouble with pastors as much as possible. The only thing wrong was that probably 50% of the time the requested permission was not forthcoming and we would never see the enquirer again — just a phone call explaining the problem, whatever it was.

This continued for quite a while, until we began to hear something of the terrible mess people were getting into because their pastors had withheld permission for ministry for them. I was filled with both sorrow and righteous anger, and the Spirit of the Lord convicted me that never again would we withhold ministry from the people of God, those who were crying out for help, on the basis of the fears of their shepherds. From that point onwards we have ministered freely in the manner of Christ and His apostles, wherever there was repentance and faith and human need. Pharisees may pass judgment but it is the judgment of the Lord that really counts, and I cannot shake the conviction that the time that remains for the cleansing and preparation of the Bride of Christ is SHORT![1]

It is certainly wise to check on an inquirer's church affiliation, and to ensure that they are under some kind of Christian authority and covering because, if they are not under any authority at all, it will be necessary for them to come under the authority of your ministry. In the normal pastoral and local church situation, there is no point in ministering deliverance to people who are not under allegiance to the Lord Jesus, first of all; and secondly, are

1 Explained fully in *End-Time Deliverance*

not also prepared to be covered by a Christian pastor or ministry and therefore **submitted to a pastoral authority,** for the purposes of their ongoing growth and strengthening as Christians.[1]

Let us now assume that a sufferer has received a pamphlet, read it, and is convicted to make further contact with you; or alternatively your earlier contact has led you to believe that there is a chance of spiritual profit, blessing and success from proceeding further.

It is time for an interview.

2. The Interview.

We can now assume that the enquirer (whether from within or outside your assembly) has made an appointment to discuss their situation with the person who can help them take the next step towards their complete spiritual renewal. If they indicate that they are "born-again" Christians, the interviewer should be one of your church's **deliverance ministers**. However, should there be some doubt about their Christian conversion, obviously the first step will be for them to talk to one of your **personal workers** who can lead them into the saving knowledge of Jesus Christ. Let me repeat again, that the blessings of the New Covenant are for those who live in the light of the New Covenant, which was ratified with Jesus' precious blood, and **I would not normally dare to minister the salvation of Jesus' blood to anyone who rejected His Lordship over their lives,** because if they persisted in their rejection, their last state would be seven times worse than their present state. In local church situations, persons who wish to receive Christ's delivering grace must first receive Christ as their Saviour and Lord. There may be exceptions to this, but only under the direct leading of the Holy Spirit (Acts 16:18), including certain evangelistic situations (Acts 8:5–13), and large group

---

1 See Book 2, Chapter 6 and Book 3, Chapter 7.

situations where the healing and delivering power of the Holy Spirit flows in sovereign grace. However, we are talking here of situations where YOU are God's agent for a FULL salvation. Thus **for unconverted people, two interviews may be necessary,** one for conversion and one for deliverance counseling — unless you have unlimited time. Each interview will bring its own blessing to the one seeking God's help.

If you only have a few people in your church seeking deliverance each year and the only people who ask for ministry are well-known to you, and you have some intimate knowledge of their problems, you may not need to be quite so methodical as I am suggesting. I am simply recording for your assistance the methods I employed, and which I found quite successful in "processing" groups of up to fifty people previously unknown to me, through effective ministry. I share with you these ideas for you to examine and employ as the Holy Spirit leads you. Spiritual PRINCIPLES are usually unchanging, but METHODS may vary, of course.

What we have shared above is useful when you only have occasional inquiries for ministry. If, however, you experience an overload of interviews, here is what we at F.S.F. do now:

1. We check if the enquirer is a Christian or wants to be a Christian.

2. We suggest they attend two ministry meetings — this will answer 90% of their questions.

The Curse Breaking prayer said by all at the beginning of our meetings will get "fringe" people into the Kingdom of God. If they come back for the second meeting, it is an indication that an interview — if they want it — will not be a waste of time.

(i) Length of Interviews

I prefer to **allow an hour** for each interview, although in some cases 40 minutes is ample. Our experience indicates that **the longer you go over the hour, the less likely your sufferer will come back for ministry**. People genuinely seeking help do not need a long interview — they know what they want. On the other hand, people who want to go into long, lurid details of their experiences, with you as a captive audience, already have what they came for — your attention, your acceptance, your sympathy etc.

Their sense of importance has been gratified and you have met their immediate need, so it is a real bonus blessing if they proceed with ministry.

(ii) Putting Them at Ease

The first few moments of the interview are spent in putting the interviewee/sufferer at ease — perhaps by offering a hot drink, or by introducing your co-interviewer. Always try to have a third person — perhaps even more than one — present at all times when interviewing strangers. When I think of some of the violent, murderous people I have interviewed alone, in the early days, I thank God for His continuing protection of me — overruling my ignorance.

I remember one occasion a member of the Irish Republican Army (I.RA.) sat down in my study and told me how he had been responsible for some bombing in Ireland, and had fled to Australia in fear of his life. Irish Loyalist agents had traced him here and he was understandably quite disturbed, although very controlled. We just concluded the introductions when my phone rang, and while I was engaged, he slipped out and away. It was strange that he should come to me — a Church of England priest — but at no time was he a personal threat to me. He wanted some kind of help — probably spiritual — but I only mention this to illustrate that when one engages in spiritual warfare regularly, one may be called upon for help by desperate and dangerous people. Very often they will know absolutely nothing about you, but the Spirit of God will cause your paths to cross. I don't have to tell you who hinders and obstructs where possible.

I wish I had a second counselor with me who could have answered the phone.

(iii) Gathering Personal Information

It is always a good idea to have another human witness at the interview, and also to be training someone in deliverance counseling. There is no way the interviewer is going to remember all the personal details of hundreds of sufferers for very long, so a **"Confidential Personal Particulars"** sheet needs to be drawn up by the interviewer. The usual things such as name, address, phone numbers, marital status, age, family makeup, are helpful; but the questions that really count are those concerned with the inquirer's background and experience, e.g.

1) Some frank answers about the relationship with father and mother:
   (a) What were your biggest problems with dad or mum?
   (b) Did you experience love, security, rejection, resentment, (as a child)?

2) Record the conversion experience briefly.

3) Any memorable experiences with the Holy Spirit?

4) What are the **worst things** that have happened to you?

5) **Medical** history (including psychiatry)?

6) **Occult** experiences?

7) **Sexual** or **personality** problems?

— and perhaps finally you can ask —

8) "What do you want the Lord to do for you?" — or to put it another way — "What are the biggest areas of failure in your Christian life?"

It may be argued that such a **"Confidential Personal Particulars"** sheet brings a psychological approach rather than a biblical approach to the problem, and that discernment is being replaced by psychology, but that is not true. When Jesus walked the earth, He asked people, "What do you want me to do for you?" (Mark 10:51), and they told Him, and He did it. All we are doing is asking people what areas in their lives do they want Jesus to attend to. Jesus once asked the father of a demonised boy, "How long has he had this?" (Mark 9:21). Whether or not Jesus knew the answer to His questions is not the point. If it is good enough for Jesus to combine discernment with counseling, then we don't need any higher authority than that.

Nowadays, with my wife, Verlie, and I working as a team, and with her taking the brunt of the deliverance work, we are able to compare (my) notes and (her) discernment.

What happens is that I may take details from the sufferer on a sheet of paper but I keep this information from Verlie unless she asks for it. Later when the time for ministry arrives, Verlie will minister by the **direct revelation of the Holy Spirit.**

(iv) Trust only the Holy Spirit!

While a sufferer will usually give you fairly accurate information about their problems, they can sometimes be wrong, especially if a marital situation is involved or they are a closet (undiagnosed) schizophrenic or paranoid. Some folk may simply be attention-seeking and invent a good story or exaggerate to satisfy their need for sympathetic attention. Others, of course, live in a fantasy-land, so when it comes down to directions for your ministry to them **you can really only trust the Holy Spirit.**

(v) A Second Witness

Verlie does not want to be influenced by my notes (what the sufferer has said) or my discernment so it is better that I tell her nothing. If, by the grace of God, she is onto something but the revelation is not complete and something is escaping her, she can tell me what she has received and we then check the notes. Most of the time these days however, she does not need to refer to my notes, and when she does, it is for confirmation only, a second witness. Praise the Lord!

(vi) Security of Personal Information

A Word of Knowledge or **discernment may well operate during the interview** — Praise the Lord! Usually those areas nominated by the Holy Spirit should be tackled first (unless it is a warning from the Spirit) and they should be carefully noted on the particulars sheet. These sheets should be treated with the utmost care and privacy in the same manner as psychiatric case histories. I find it safer to detach the name, address and phone number from the personal particulars and use a code system to tie them in together again when necessary. In that way no one can tie up the identification of the sufferer with their personal details except yourself, thus removing any security risk. This is especially important if you do not have a lockable steel filing cabinet or safe. Perhaps even better than a steel cabinet or safe could be a Personal Computer with a security program that requires a password to unlock it before it divulges all its highly confidential information. The point is, you are responsible for the TOTAL SECURITY of ANY RECORDED information!

(vii) What to Reveal

One further point on words of knowledge and discerning of spirits. These are two very precious gifts, of course, and vital for continuously successful ministry; and having been given knowledge or discernment, or both, **one needs the wisdom of Christ to know what to reveal to the sufferer**. They usually need to know SOMETHING of what the Lord has revealed to you in order that they might be encouraged. However, **one should NOT reveal what will DISCOURAGE**. There is plenty of time for that when they are in a stronger spiritual condition. **Beware of parading the knowledge or discernment received by you**. The Word of God tells us that "**a fool reveals all of his spirit, but a wise man controls and quiets it.**" (Prov. 29:11 – lit. Heb.).

You may feel some fleshly desire to be accepted by the sufferer, or you may harbour a hidden fear of your ministry being rejected by *them*. This is particularly true in deliverance work, of which there has been much rejection up to the present time. Whatever the situation, it is helpful to remember that you are only the LORD'S REPRESENTATIVE and that you are not there to impress them with yourself, so be sure to resist the temptation to show off your spirituality and appear clever. *They need to know only enough to indicate that the Lord knows them intimately, and cares, and is already on the job of beginning to put them right*, and that you are the servant through whom the Lord is working. If you parade your gifts and take glory for yourself by revealing too much at once, you will probably frighten the sufferer away (the unclean spirits will certainly take fright) and never see them again. There is no prize for guessing who is the winner in such cases.

The "problem" is that the Lord is very likely to reveal something to the minister which, should you reveal it to the sufferer, may not be acknowledged by them as one of their problem areas. They are aware of SOME of the truth about their inner selves but certainly not all of it. The Lord may have given you (the minister) **the truth behind the truth.**

Should you reveal such discernment to the sufferer they could be frightened, they could be impressed or they could think you are a blithering idiot who does not know what you are talking about. It is amazing just how many demonised people who are in great need seem to think they know more about the deliverance ministry than the deliverance minister does.

They think to themselves "I know me better than you do", and that would be right if it were not for the Holy Spirit, but of course He knows the sufferer better than the sufferer knows himself. Most people know their big problems, their obvious, visible problems, but **not many know what is lurking deep and hidden within them, where the strong (man) dwells.**

This may be the best place to illustrate a great error I once made. Two precious Christian friends of mine once asked me to interview a couple who had experienced a series of minor and major disasters in their family life. As a result these folk, who were considered quite mature in faith, were seeking the Lord to discover if there was any particular source in their lives from which these continuing spiritual and physical attacks were being mounted against them. A special appointment was made at my friends' home and we gathered together. To cut a long story short, the couple each gave an account of their misadventures, but during my questions which followed, I noticed the wife was becoming angry in spirit and a whole range of problems within her were given to me by the Lord.

At the end of the questioning I was asked for an opinion, but I felt most reluctant to say anything because I sensed in my spirit that it would not be received, and only increase the anger. However I was pressed to say something because I was accused of being evasive (which I was) with the inference that the whole interview would have been a waste of time. The Lord then gave me the wisdom to offer discernment of one key problem in the woman to see how she could cope with it, **but as it was not the answer she wanted**, the anger flared quickly and I could see that it would be wiser to say the minimum and retire out of the situation as gracefully and as quickly as possible, but leaving the door open for the future — which I did. The ministry was flatly rejected (politely, under stress) and I was told there was no possibility of my ministering further because I was not trusted, and she would seek counseling elsewhere. My friends who had arranged the meeting, later told me that they had honestly thought that the couple were ready to go ahead seriously and were sorry for wasting my time.

In fact, my time was not wasted. I learned several important lessons:

1)   Do not be a party to an interview **set up by a third party** UNLESS there is no other way. If the sufferers are interested and desperate enough, **they will make their OWN approach and appointment!**

2)   Always ensure that interviews are **in the strictest confidence for all parties**. The wife threatened to take my brief comments and discernment into the next interview they obtained with another minister, and I am sure that, taken out of accurate context, they would have been presented unconvincingly, and perhaps disparagingly, to put it mildly. It is interesting how some sufferers expect ministers to treat interviews in strict confidence, but they themselves "talk their heads off" about what the minister said.

3)   **Don't share too much** of what the Lord gives you — the interviewee does not need to know everything straight away; in fact it will almost certainly be counter-productive. I was very glad the Lord had cautioned me to venture discernment on only one area of spiritual warfare in their lives.

4)   If the situation becomes uncooperative and unprofitable, close the interview as quickly and as graciously as possible, but try to leave the door open for future contact. The convicting work of the Spirit can, and does, work miracles

in breaking down hostility and enabling people to face up to the truth.

5)　Afterwards I was a little surprised the Lord did not lead me into **a direct confrontation with the spirit of anger,** but His ways are higher than ours and it is doubtful if PARTIAL ministry would have changed the human will, the attitude of which is so important for thorough cleansing. The next section may help to clarify this.

3. Trust, Submission and Cooperation.

By the time the interview is half-completed, the sufferer will know whether or not the Interviewer has the love of Jesus in his or her heart, and is truly a minister of Jesus. Some of the areas of difficulty you will be talking about will be very personal and private to the sufferer, so if they are in any way cautious or untrusting, it will soon show in their unwillingness to talk or give answers. There may be some basic evasiveness if they themselves are unwilling to admit certain problems, but as trust grows (and it is trust in Jesus in you) embarrassment can be overcome and important background information emerge.

The sufferer has to be brought to the position where there is:

(a)　**trust in the counselor/minister** as a true servant of Jesus;

(b)　submission to the Christian authority of the counselor/minister over the life of the sufferer — **in all matters relative to the ministry of deliverance,** and flowing from these,

(c)　the full cooperation of the sufferer during deliverance battle sessions which at times may amount to **unquestioned obedience.** When we say unquestioned obedience, we mean **obey first and ask questions afterwards** if necessary. It the sufferer wants all the answers before he or she will obey, then obviously there is no trust; no recognition of a pastoral authority and no cooperation — all of which adds up to "no deal" as far as the counselor/minister is concerned.

Sometimes people will say to you "I trust Jesus but I don't know so much about you. Where does it say I have to trust you in the Bible?"

Such a challenge is sometimes genuine and **sometimes inspired by a religious spirit** wanting to parade its "spirituality". We have all met Christians who carry the "I look only to Jesus — not man" truth to the point where they reject any form of valid Christian or pastoral authority over them. **They use the Lord to justify their rebellion** in such a way that they cannot be straightened out — except by a discerning deliverance minister.

However one answer to the challenge is found in 2 Corinthians 8:5 where Paul commends the Macedonians for **trusting Christ FIRST "AND US (apostles) BY THE WILL OF GOD!"** It is made perfectly clear that the trusting of God's genuine servants (after first trusting Christ) **is the Will of God**. That way they could receive the blessings that the Lord had in store for them. See also Exod. 4:16, 7:1, Gal. 4:14, Heb. 13:17.

There will always be the situation where persons brought to you by relatives or friends will be **mentally incapable** of seeking help, let alone contributing the things we have just discussed. In such cases you must be led by the Holy Spirit but it is necessary to enlist the full cooperation of at **least one relative or friend**. The Salvation of Jesus Christ operates in our lives by FAITH/TRUST and you will normally need to perceive that such faith is present one way or another in order that the promises of God may be appropriated. However, there may be **fairly unusual situations** where the Holy Spirit convicts you to exercise YOUR OWN faith in order to achieve the desired result (e.g. Acts 16:18).

FELLOWSHIP AND TEACHING

I have always insisted that people seeking deliverance attend Christian meetings (church) where Christian praise and teaching are staple diet for the human spirit and soul. As the kingdom of darkness is torn down in the soul by the ministry of deliverance, it needs to be replaced by the Kingdom of God, or the last state of the person may be seven times worse than the first. As the **unclean spirits** are torn out so they must be replaced by the **Holy Spirit** of God. **It is absolutely vital that the person seeking deliverance accept their need for Christian fellowship and teaching** in order that they may be strengthened in the things of God and not left an empty vacuum, because they won't be permitted to remain empty for very long.

Again, it is a waste of time and spiritual power setting people free from the powers of darkness if they decline to follow your directions, assuming that your directions are in accord with what the New Testament directs for the sanctification and conduct of growing Christians. **A Deliverance and Restoration program has three (3) essential foundations.** They are:

(i)   Deliverance ministry
(ii) Bible Teaching
(iii) True discipleship

I think it is very important to let the sufferer know what the Lord (through you) expects of them.

We will say more about the need for TRUST during the ongoing warfare, at a later stage.[1]

---

1 Chapter 8, "Opposition", Book 3

4. Permission to Minister

(i) Overcoming a Change of Heart/Mind

An enquirer should be warned that, once deliverance starts, their minds will probably think up a dozen good reasons why they should stop having ministry. The enemy in the soul will induce certain feelings of reluctance, etc. and the emotions will be put into action against the ministry. This is one of those situations where the emotions must be put down and ignored because they will be inspired by the unclean. **The emotions must be put down and overruled by decisions of the will**. Decisions of the will can be made according to the known will of God as revealed in the Word of God, and **these must be adhered to if the sufferer is to win the battle. Sufferers should beware of emotions or "feelings"**, especially when receiving deliverance.

Following on from this, it is possible to have people inquire for ministry who will plead earnestly for help, and who promise they will do ANYTHING you say because they need help so desperately, and later on what is in them has turned them completely against you. They will deny almost everything they ever told you and say, "Who gave you the authority or permission to minister to me?" — and you know how satan loves to scandalize and slander Christian leaders. He'll have your name draped all over the front page of the Press and the demons in your sufferer will be screaming: "Negligence! Personal bodily harm — I'll sue!, etc". The world and half the Church will think you are a blithering idiot (you may have to pay that price anyway), and other potential enquirers will be filled with alarm. The latter may never again think of Jesus' deliverance as a possible answer to their desperate needs, and all because a satanic agency has twisted the truth, and other undiscerning Christians, including leaders, accept every critical word. **There is something unclean inside most of us that loves to hear criticism of other ministries, especially effective anointed ministries**; so that when an unclean spirit speaks up and complains of them, instead of discerning it and telling it to be silent and come out in Jesus' Name, we say, "Tut, tut, isn't that terrible. WE would never treat you like that!"

Suppose your church had a notable visiting preacher or prophet who brought you some strange, new, powerful and authoritative teaching, and someone in your church stood up and said "**What have we** (Australians) **to do with you** (say, Pastor Smith of the U.S.A.)? **Have you come to destroy us** (by teaching us heresy and damaging our Christian faith}?" — probably half the assembly would say, "Praise the Lord, someone is speaking up against this new teaching!"

Then the interjector adds, "**I know who you are** — God's anointed for healing God's people!" — and it would be the turn of the other half of the assembly to say, "Hallelujah and amen!"

How many Christians could have discerned whether or not the speaker was simply expressing a strong Christian opinion under the guidance of the Holy Spirit, or was inspired by an unclean spirit? When we study Luke 4:31–37 carefully, we realize that the interjector's words in that incident could have been interpreted by those in the synagogue **in several different ways,** most of them quite reasonable, **but Jesus perceived the unclean spirit behind them and acted accordingly.**

(ii) A Possible Solution to Avoid Slander

What can we do today, to prevent unclean spirits carrying deception, distortion and slander from one ministry to another? I think a good deal of trouble can be eliminated from the outset by *OBTAINING FROM SUFFERERS YOU DISCERN TO BE DESTRUCTIVE*, their permission to minister IN WRITING — BEFORE you minister. This may not always be possible, but I think in today's vindictive, unbalanced world, the controlled group ministry situation needs to be exactly that, with the Pastor "calling the shots" and exercising a wise and Godly authority. The counselor/minister needs to protect himself from lies and slander **whenever possible,** and if the destructive sufferer is incapable, then the permission of the next-of-kin should be obtained. If the sufferer has been referred to you by a psychiatrist, then you should add the notation, "Referred by Dr. Bloggs, 10/10/84" across the permission slip, a possible form of which is illustrated in Appendix C.

Sincere people will have no difficulty in giving you written permission, especially if you assure them of the private confidentiality of the ministry; and **as a last resort** you can also assure them that, on completion of the ministry, for any reason whatever, you will burn or delete their file in front of their eyes, **at their request. Never, Never, Never,** return or give your private notes to a sufferer — they are not only sinners, but some of them will be confused, and others destructive towards you. Otherwise — no signature? — No ministry! Un-biblical? We need to remember that the New Testament was written in an age when the reality of demons was NOT questioned. Today there is widespread ignorance of their existence — even in the Church, but the scriptures do warn us to be as wise as serpents and as harmless as doves! Remember also, we are concerned about strangers unknown to you. Members of your own flock and those who manifest unclean activity during a meeting may present a different situation.

At the close of the interview the minister has to make a decision, and the sufferer (or those caring for the sufferer) has to make a decision, whether to proceed into ministry or not. The interview is valuable if only for the encouragement of the sufferer — ("At last — someone who understands and can really help — Praise the Lord!") Usually the decision taken will be clear-cut and mutual, one way or the other. Are you happy with the sufferer's attitude and commitment — or not? Are they happy for you to minister to them? **You need two YESSES in order to proceed.**

On rare occasions a sufferer may first like to come to your

church meetings of praise and worship and meet a few people being helped. Any lingering suspicions and doubts (that are not unclean) will quickly be dispelled by the number of shining faces in the congregation. Certainly there will be many who are still heavily oppressed and will look it; but even some of them will be transported out of themselves and into heavenly places during the meetings, because there is nothing quite like the end of a meeting of people who are experiencing the delivering power of God in their lives and who are thanking and praising God for all His goodness.

In the final analysis, the sufferer MUST TRUST the minister (the Christ in you) **even more than his or her own judgment**. The mental judgment of the sufferer will almost certainly be distorted or clouded by uncleanness, but the judgment of the minister should be more in the Spirit and in truth.

(iii) Hatred

We have said some difficult things in this section, in relation to the attitude of the sufferer to the minister, e.g.

1) **exercise of the human will in right and Godly decisions should overrule the negative (mixed-up) emotions;**

2) trust, submission and cooperation should be at the level where **the minister's judgment should be obeyed and followed in preference to the sufferer's own inclinations or judgments.**

I'm sure I do not have to repeat the reason why the sufferer's judgment in spiritual matters will suffer distortion. In fact, as soon as a mutual decision is made to proceed with ministry, I make a practice of warning the sufferer that somewhere along the way they are going to HATE me and/or my wife Verlie, who has become our top deliverance minister. They usually laugh at the time, but it is often true. As soon as the ministry begins to penetrate deeply into the kingdoms of darkness in the soul, that ugly part of the personality gets really stirred up and the spirit of hatred emerges from his hiding place. There are no prizes for guessing the object of his attention. Of course, if the sufferer does NOT trust you more than their own judgments or emotions, hatred will take them away and their deliverance will be lost, the consequences of which may be utterly disastrous for them. Also, they will proceed to slander your name at every opportunity throughout the church and the world.

However, praise God, if your sufferer is forewarned, when hatred does stick his neck out, you can join forces together in lopping his head off (metaphorically) and afterwards have a Godly laugh about it together. NOW do you understand how important it is that they first trust Jesus, and then you as Jesus' minister?

At this point, like any professional soldier, we should be thoroughly prepared, ready for spiritual battle, and in position.

Book 2 is appropriately entitled: "ENGAGING THE ENEMY".

PERSONAL NOTE FROM THE AUTHOR

Thank you for buying this book.

You may not realize it but every Christian in the West who buys a book published by Full Salvation Fellowship (most written by myself) enables this work of God to send a similar book to the mission field in the east — India, Philippines, Africa, Asia etc.

One of the great miracles of today is the way in which this work, raised up in our little home in 1979, has kept a Pastor and his family, rented a Hall and funded a publishing program — all from the tithes and thank-offerings of a small group of needy people, most of whom are on welfare or pensions.

I know WHO has done it, but I still don't know HOW He has done it! Praise His Holy Name!

As I sit here meditating on this, I realize that we can't ask a man for money for a book who is unable to feed his children, but we are charged with the mission to GET THE MESSAGE OUT! QUICK! — to the Body of Christ world-wide.

Thanks again, in Jesus' Name, for buying our books. We believe it will be a blessing to you — and you are helping us to bring that blessing to others.

Thank you, brother and sister, thank you.

Peter Hobson
Sydney, August1991
January 2014

PS: Any further assistance you wish to make can be sent to:

Full Salvation Fellowship Ltd.
P.O. Box 1020
CROWS NEST, NSW 2065
AUSTRALIA

— please indicate which nation you wish to benefit from your missionary contribution.

APPENDIX A

THE BIBLE'S CONDEMNATION OF THE OCCULT

Deut. 18:9–14. "When you come into the land which the Lord your God gives you, you shall not learn to follow the abominable practices of those nations. There shall not be found among you anyone who burns his son or his daughter as an offering, any one who practices **divination**, a **soothsayer**, or an **augur**, or a **sorcerer**, or a **charmer**, or a **medium**, or a **wizard**, or a **necromancer**. For **whoever does these things is an abomination to the Lord**; and because of these abominable practices the Lord your God is driving them out before you. You shall be blameless before the Lord your God. For these nations, which you are about to dispossess, give heed to soothsayers and to diviners; but as for you, the Lord your God has not allowed you so to do".

Acts 16:16–18. "As we were going to the place of prayer, we were met by a slave girl who had a spirit of divination (a python) and brought her owners much gain by soothsaying. She followed Paul and us, crying, These men are servants of the Most High God, who proclaim to you the way of salvation'. And this she did for many days. But Paul was annoyed, and turned and said to the spirit, 'I charge you in the name of Jesus Christ to come out of her'. And it came out that very hour".

Isaiah 47:9–13. "These two things shall come to you in a moment, in one day; the loss of children and widowhood shall come upon you in full measure, in spite of your many sorceries and the great power of your enchantments. You felt secure in your wickedness, you said, 'No one sees me'; **your wisdom and your**

knowledge led you astray, and you said in your heart, 'I am, and there is no one besides me'. But **evil** shall come upon you, for which you cannot atone; **disaster** shall fall upon you, which you will not be able to expiate; and ruin shall come on you suddenly, of which you know nothing. Stand fast in your enchantments and your many sorceries, with which you labored from your youth; perhaps you may be able to succeed, perhaps you may inspire terror. You are wearied with your many counsels; let them stand forth and save you, those who divide the heavens, who gaze at the stars, who at the new moons predict what shall befall you" (cf. 1 Thess. 5:2–3).

2 Kings 17:17–18. "And they burned their sons and their daughters as offerings, and used **divination** and **sorcery**, and sold themselves to do **evil** in the sight of the Lord, provoking him to anger. Therefore the Lord was very angry with Israel, and removed them out of his sight; none was left but the tribe of Judah only".

Lev.19:31. "Do not turn to **mediums** or **wizards**; do not seek them out, to be defiled by them: I am the Lord your God".

2 Thess. 2:7–12. "For the mystery of lawlessness is already at work; only he who now restrains it will do so until he is out of the way. And then the lawless one will be revealed, and the Lord Jesus will slay him with the breath of his mouth and destroy him by his appearing and his coming. The coming of the lawless one by the activity of satan will be with **all power** and with **pretended signs and wonders**, and with **all wicked deception** for those who are to perish, because they refused to love the truth and so be saved.

Therefore God sends upon them **a strong delusion**, to make them believe what is false, so that all may be condemned who did not believe the truth but had pleasure in unrighteousness".

Also, read: 1 Samuel 28; Isa. 8:19–22; Malachi 3:5; Exod. 22:18; Micah 5:12; Acts 19:18–20 and Rev. 13:12–15.

APPENDIX B

SUGGESTED INTRODUCTORY PAMPHLET

"SO YOU THINK YOU NEED DELIVERANCE?"

Well, you probably do: let's discuss it. You need to know if you have a need for the help of the deliverance ministry of Jesus Christ and whether you can put into operation in your life the necessary steps to obtain your deliverance and freedom.

THE PROBLEM

When we speak of deliverance, of course, we are talking about deliverance from oppression or bondage from unclean spirits or demons — supernatural personalities that are the beggarly and elemental spirits of the universe mentioned by the Apostle Paul. The Apostle John says that **the whole world lies in (the power of) the evil one** (satan) and he exercises his power throughout the world by the "rulers and authorities of darkness" which are some of the terms the Bible uses to describe evil supernatural personalities.

These spirits can oppress you from within someone's human body, such as a person living across the street; from within your own body or from within a house or area you live in but outside your own body. Most people being oppressed know or at least sense what is their own need, especially after having tried various other methods of treatment without success. God's answer is that He sent His Son Jesus Christ to bleed and die on a Cross that you might be set free: "… nailing it to the Cross. **He disarmed the principalities and powers** and made a public example of them, **triumphing over them** in it (the Cross)" (Colossians 2:15).

In this world then, we are all subjected in some degree to the influence of evil — there are no exceptions. That is why Christ came — to save us from our sins and from our bondage to evil. **"The reason the Son of God was manifested was to destroy (loose) the works of the devil"** (1 John 3:8) — but let us make quite clear right now that to obtain Jesus' help, you have to trust Him completely. If you cannot put your trust in Him as your Saviour and Lord, it is better that you do not commence receiving deliverance because you may deteriorate rather than improve. According to the Bible, early successes may be reversed and your condition regress (Matthew 12:43–45). You cannot belong to satan AND to Christ. You cannot be a member of the Kingdom of satan and the Kingdom of God. To quote the words of Joshua: **"Choose you this day whom you will serve** ... but for me and my house, we will serve the Lord!" (Joshua 24:15).

THE COVENANT

We need to remember that deliverance is a MAJOR benefit of the New Covenant. But you may ask, "What does this word 'Covenant' mean?" It simply means testament or agreement, and for the Christian it carries both blessings and responsibilities. The Bible is a record of two covenants or testaments — the Old Testament which operated until the Lord Jesus Christ introduced and ratified the New Covenant or Testament with His own precious blood, shed on the Cross. In other words, Christ has obtained a new deal for people seeking God and we can find out all about it by reading the New Testament of the Bible. In brief, this new deal is like a narrow path up the side of a mountain. There are all sorts of side-tracks leading off the narrow path, which God has marked "DANGER". While we keep to God's path of the New Covenant for our lives, we can safely negotiate our way through this world until we receive our inheritance in Glory. However, satan has marked all the dangerous side-tracks with HIS sign-posts such as "Permissive Pleasure" — "Occult Truth" — "Power through Politics" — "Gods of Eastern Mysticism" —"Healing through Hypnosis" — "Sexual Liberty" — "Do your own Thing," etc. but which in fact lead to slavery, darkness and destruction (Matt. 7:13–20).

So the restrictions of the New Testament upon our lives **are for our own good** — our health and safety. By trust and obedience we can negotiate this life in peace and security in spite of the beggarly and elemental spirits of the universe. To stray into the side-tracks, however, brings us into disobedience against God and out from under Jesus' protection, exposing us to the fiery attacks of evil. Our footing gives way and we tumble down into blackness. Are YOU in need of help? Praise God, Jesus remains our way of escape and we can return to God's way by becoming a more informed Christian on the subject of the New Covenant, and the full salvation the Lord Jesus has obtained **for those who believe.**

If you are someone who needs to consider becoming a Christian as your first step, I can assure you that if you put your trust in the Lord Jesus and accept His unconditional Lordship over your life, endeavoring to keep the Covenant as obediently and faithfully as you can, then **nothing on earth or beyond** can stop you from being delivered of your oppression as you seek the help of the deliverance ministry of Christ. Contact the writer if you want to become a Christian or re-dedicate your life to Christ, and you have no mature Christian friends available to help you.

DELIVERANCE FOR CHRISTIANS

The more we are involved with Christ, the more He is "involved" with us to deliver us, and many problems of a demonic character may be eliminated simply by Christian growth and faithfulness. Healing prayer, too, will be successful in many cases. However, there are also many other cases where a problem remains to the extent that it becomes a BARRIER to Christian growth, **actually preventing a closer relationship with the Lord**; and when prayer for healing appears unsuccessful, it is at this point that the specific ministry of deliverance usually becomes necessary for the individual Christian if progress towards Christlikeness is to be continued.

It is important to remember that the Lord doesn't want you to receive just a portion of His Covenantal promises, but He wants to shower upon you ALL His blessings as given to us in the New Covenant. As we said earlier, the WHOLE Covenant, **with all its blessings and responsibilities** is YOURS, IF you are prepared to deny yourself, take up your Cross and follow Jesus.

If, for a variety of genuine reasons (such as you are a new Christian) you do not have pastoral care at the moment, you must be prepared to accept oversight from the Ministers of Full Salvation Fellowship, if only on a temporary basis, and submit to their pastoral guidance. Failure to do this simply means that receiving ministry is a waste of time and better not undertaken in the first place. We are too busy to play games in matters of good and evil, life and death.

We trust that you now have something of an idea as to the place of the deliverance ministry in the total ministry of the Church and perhaps in your life. This is only an introduction, of course, to enable you to clarify your thinking. Don't be afraid — have faith in God and in His Son the Lord Jesus, for the victory has already been won - Praise the Lord!

Yours in Christ's service,

FULL SALVATION FELLOWSHIP

APPENDIX C

(FOR ILLUSTRATIVE PURPOSES ONLY):
CONFIDENTIAL DECLARATION OF INTENTION

DATE: _____ NAME: _____

PHONE: _____ ADDRESS: _____

Of my own free will I now wish to receive Christian Ministry at _____ and I understand that no LEGAL responsibility can be accepted for my well-being. I desire to submit to Christ's ministry and agree to follow the advice received from His counselors under the Pastor's authority. I seek healing in order to serve the Lord Jesus as He leads me:

Signed _____

While no legal responsibility is accepted by the ministers, it is well to remind our sufferers that we are responsible for them before the Lord, **provided they follow our pastoral directions.** We accept no legal responsibility because the civil laws have no cognizance of spiritual things. Because of ignorance, human justice can be perverted by unclean spirits. Not so with Almighty God. He knows the truth and **He knows who is responsible**, and it is before Him we are all accountable in the end. Thus we are MORALLY responsible to God, in part, for every human being GENUINELY requesting help, and for the right use of the ministry entrusted to us.

As suggested in this book, this kind of authorization is especially desirable when you are informed or discern that the sufferer is DESTRUCTIVE.

APPENDIX D

BIBLE NOTES ON DEMONOLOGY

1. **The Enemy — Satan or Devil — The Prince or Ruler of Demons (Matt. 12:24):**

   Other titles: Isaiah 14:12, Matt. 12:24, John 12:31, 2 Cor. 4:4, Eph. 2:2, 6:12, Rev. 12:10.

   Background and Future: Gen. 3:14–15, Isa. 14:12–19, Matt. 25:41, Luke 10:18, Rev. 12:7–12, 20:1–10.

   Character and Works: Gen. 3:1, Exodus 12, Matt. 18:34, 4:3, John 8:44, 2 Cor. 11:14, Eph. 2:2, 2 Thess.2:9–10, 1 Peter 5:8, 1 John 3:8, Rev. 9:11, 12:10.

   Metaphors, or forms used for Satan: Dragon, serpent, Leviathan – Isaiah 27:1 etc.

   Treatment of the Devil: Luke 10:19, 4:1–13, Matt. 4:1–11, James 4:7–8, Jude 9.

2. **Satan's Army:**

   Angels: Matt. 25:41, Luke 10:17–18, Rev.12:7–9.

   demons: Luke 10:17–18.

   spirits of demons: Luke 4:33, Rev. 16:14. (Check literal translation)

   } Eph.6:11–12

3. Personality of demons:

They have **Knowledge** – Mark 5:7, Matt. 8:29, Acts 16:17.

Will – Matt. 12:44, Mark 5:10–12.

Emotion – Matt. 12:43, 8:28, Mark 5:7, Mark 5:10,12.

4. Works of demons:

Sin: Gen. 4:7 (lit.), 1 Kings 22:19–23, Hosea 3:4, 4:12, Matt. 12:38–45, Eph. 2:2, 6:12, Rev. 18:2–5.

False teaching: Acts 13:8–10, 2 Cor. 11:3–4, 1 Tim. 4:1–2, James 3:14–16, 1 John 4:1–3.

Corruption of worship: Levit. 17:7, Deut. 32:17, Psalm 106:36–38, 1 Cor. 10:20–21, Gal. 4:3–9, Rev. 9:20.

Deceiving miracles: Matt. 24:24, Acts 16:16, 2 Thess. 2:1–10.

Physical/Mental sickness: Luke 8:35, 9:39, 13:11, Matt. 12:22 (cf. Matt. 9:32–33, 17:15, Mark 5:4–5, 9:17–25).

5. The Sovereignty of God over demons:

1 Sam. 16:14–15, 18:10, 1 Kings 22:21–23, Psalm 78:49–50, Luke 8:28–33, 1 Cor. 15:24–28.

6. The Victory of Christ over demons:

Matt. 8:16–17, Col. 2:13–15, 1 Peter 3:21–22, 1 John 3:8.

7. This Victory given to the Church:

Rom. 8:38–39, Eph. 3:10, 6:12.
(Also 1 Cor. 6:2–3, 2 Cor. 10:3–6, James 4:7, 1 John 4:4).

8. Authority the key:

Jesus: Matt. 8:5–10, 16–17, 28:18, Mark 1:22, 27, 1 Cor. 15:27–28, Phil. 3:20, 1 Peter 3:22, etc.

Disciples: Matt. 9:37, 10:1, 5–9, 17:18–20, 18:18–22, 28:19–20, Luke 9:1–2, 10:17–19, 17:5–6, John 20:21, Mark 11:19–25.

Believers: Mark 9:23, 16:17–18, John 14:12–14.

Binding and Loosing: Matt. 18:18, Luke 13:10–17, Mark 3:20–27, (cf. Mark 11:12–14, 20–25, 1 Tim. 1:20, Acts 5:1–11, 13:6–12, 1 Cor. 5:1–5).

Christians' Feet: Gen. 3:15, Josh. 10:24, Luke 10:19, Rom. 16: 19–20, Eph. 6:13–16. (See *Christian Authority and Power* Appendix for a full study).

Appendix E

Breaking Curses

PRAYER OF RENUNCIATION (Forsaking/Rejection)

Greeting and Identification
Dear Lord Jesus ...

Choosing your King/Kingdom
I renounce the devil and all his works. I renounce the powers of darkness and all their works, and I acknowledge you, Lord Jesus Christ, to be my Lord and my God. (2 Cor. 4:2, Eph. 6:12, Rom. 1:21, John 20:28)

Breaking the Chains:
I ask you to break every chain which binds me; remove from me every foul curse that has been laid upon my life, even to the third and fourth generation, and before that if necessary. I now take my authority and break every curse upon me, in the name of Jesus of Nazareth, because Jesus became accursed for me. I thank you dear Lord for this authority and this power to break every curse. (Job 36:5–11, Acts 12:7, Heb. 13:3, 1 John 3:8, Ex. 20:5, Luke 10:19, Gal. 3:13, Luke 24:49, Acts 1:8)

Inner Cleansing:

I ask you to take out of my heart every root of bitterness, unforgiveness and unbelief, indeed every unclean thing that hinders me from leading a Godly life. (Heb. 12:15, Matt. 6:12–15, Heb. 3:12, 2 Cor. 7:1).

I forgive – please forgive:

I forgive those who have hurt me and grieved me in the past, and I ask you to forgive them also, even as you have forgiven me, and bring us all into your full salvation. (Matt. 6:12–15, Matt. 18:21–35, Heb. 2:3).

Commitment + direction:

And now gracious Lord I yield my life into your hands. Heal me and cleanse me: deliver me and restore me: and make me like the Son of God. (Luke 9:23–26, John 3:16, Jer. 17:14, Ps. 107:19–20, Ps. 51:10, 1 John 1:7–9, Ps. 41:1–3, Acts 3:21, Rom. 8:29, 2 Cor. 3:18, 1 Cor. 11:1, 1 John 3:2–3).

Thanksgiving:

Thank you Lord Jesus. (Eph. 5:4, Col. 2:7). Amen

Recommendations from Readers...

"We are enjoying your books which give such a **practical approach** to this ministry ... We would welcome some affiliation with you ... as there is no (other) Fellowship in Israel engaged in Deliverance."

Alan and Helena Friedman,
Jerusalem

... **expounds scripture** capably to show the enormous need and scope of deliverance ministry in these end times ... **detailed guidelines are provided** for Ministers whom God has prompted to begin a thorough and systematic deliverance program. You'll probably find this book will excite your desire for righteousness to fever pitch.

Steve Bewlay, Springwood A.O.G.
N.S.W., Australia

And encouragement from an unexpected source for deliverance minister (Mrs) Verlie Hobson, and for all the criminals who have accepted Christ as their Savior and Lord while in jail, but found it so difficult to go on in the Faith after their release into the world.

"That woman knows what she's doing."

Ex-lifer Darcy Dugan at a
Deliverance and Restoration meeting, July '88

PETER HOBSON BOOKS

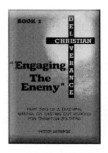

0947252029

ENGAGING THE ENEMY, VOL. 2

This second book in Peter's Deliverance Series deals with such topics as: Instructions to Demons, Commanding Spirits, Names & Discernment of Spirits, Talking With Demons, Where to Send Demons, The Transference of Spirits, Manifestations and the Lord's Answer, Self-Deliverance, & more!

0947252037

WALKING IN VICTORY, VOL. 3

This third book in Peter's Deliverance Series deals with the Battle Tactics of the Enemy, Teaching on Maintaining Deliverance, Teaching on Prayer Weapons, Forgiveness, Protection of the Blood, the Fullness of The Holy Spirit, Prosperity, Teaching on Fellowship, Worship & Praise, and more!

0947252142

WE ALL HAVE OUR DEMONS!, VOL. 4

This fourth book in Peter's Deliverance Series deals with Mind Control, Multiple Personality Disorder, Hearing Voices, Dissociate Identity Disorder, and False Memory Syndrome. Includes examples of deliverance from various spirits including fear, stupidity, rebellion, Epilepsy, superstition, blasphemy, bitterness, murder, anger, lust, pride, gluttony, the spirit of death and deliverance from cancer.

0947252150

MENTAL ILLNESS - WHAT CAN CHRISTIANS DO?

Christian ministers are facing ever increasing challenges today as they seek to help the damaged and afflicted, and never has the saving and healing grace of Jesus been more widely and obviously needed. We need to learn how to restore the human mind, soul and the body from all the damage of the enemy. Find the path to victory!

0947252088

SEX, DEMONS & MORALITY

Millions of people throughout the world have never been taught to exercise responsible restraint in their sex lives, totally misusing the enormous gift entrusted to them by a loving God. The good news is that there is a way of escape, for all those enslaved by lusts. Peter Hobson exposes the spiritual forces at work behind lusts and shows how to rid yourself and to elude their clutches in the future.

0947252061

END-TIME DELIVERANCE & THE HOLY SPIRIT REVIVAL

This book ties Jesus' ministry of deliverance with the need for cleaning house in the Church to prepare the Bride for His return. Peter covers: the Magnitude of Human Demonization, God's Unfolding Plan of Continual Deliverance, Healing & Discernment, the End-Time Deliverance Ministry, and more!

www.impactchristianbooks.com
1-800-451-2708

PETER HOBSON BOOKS (CONT)

0947252045

YOUR FULL SALVATION

Whoever you are - wherever you are - this book will give you the direction you need in your life to be ready for Christ's return! Through his studies in the Bible, Peter Hobson has discovered that evangelism, healing and deliverance were part of the Saviourhood of our Lord Jesus. And they are all an effective part of God's end-time plan!

0947252126

RELIGIOUS SPIRITS: THE BLIGHT IN THE CHURCHES

Find the harm that religious spirits can do - and are doing - in our churches today. Peter addresses: religion vs. Christianity, religious spirits in the Churches, Pharisaism, Dangers in the Renewal Movement, Counterfeits of the Name Above Every Name, and more!

0947252096

GUIDANCE FOR THOSE RECEIVING DELIVERANCE

This book meets the needs and questions of someone seeking deliverance. It discusses: Interpreting symptoms, Prayer and Restoration, the Christian armor, Discretion, and Opposition from the Church and the World to Deliverance.

www.impactchristianbooks.com
1-800-451-2708

094725210X

SURVIVING THE DISTRESS OF NATIONS

A Peter Hobson booklet on End Time events and signs. He explains what a person can do to be prepared for the soon coming of Jesus Christ. Specific Topics include: The End of This Age (Israel, Weather Changes, Pole Shifts, Earthquakes, etc), Details of the End of the World, Warning Signs - Pestilences & Plagues, Stockmarket, Ozone Levels, Identity Cards, Crime, Famine, Pollution, and God's Solution.

094725207X

HEADCOVERING AND LADY PASTORS & TEACHERS

A sensitive treatment of this delicate subject. Peter Hobson discusses the *for* and *against* of head covering in the Church today. He includes topics on the Relationship between men and women, the Relevance of Paul's teaching for today, Reasons for head covering, Opposing views to head covering, and the Appointment of women and lady pastors/ teachers. A must for anyone with questions!

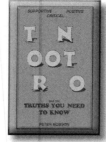

0947252118

TORONTO - THE TRUTHS YOU NEED TO KNOW

"Probably the most vigorous and definitive defense - and criticism - of the Toronto Blessing yet published." This book explains WHY the Toronto experience began and WHERE it will inevitably lead for those who have been praying and expecting the Lord to move powerfully through the Church.

BEWARE HYPOCRISY! THE CASE FOR TRUE RENEWAL...

0947252169

The purpose of this book is to turn Bible-loving Christian from being unintended Hypocrites into True Disciples of Jesus Christ - for the challenging days ahead!

What do you think is a good description of a Christian who (rightly) opposes homosexual practice because it is against the Word of God, but then explains away as out of date the two full chapters on the right use of tongues and prophecy (1 Cor. 12 & 14)? Hypocrite?

How would you describe a "Bible-believing Christian" leader who opposes Christ's command to heal the sick and cast out demons, essential ministries of the Great Commission with which the Lord has charged His Church? Pharisee? False teacher? Rebel? Scatterer (wolf) - Matt. 12:30? If we are not with Him we are against Him - said Jesus after healing the blind and dumb demoniac.

CHRISTIAN AUTHORITY, POWER, AND THE STIGMATA

0947252053

Ever read a study so power-packed with revelations of God that it kept you in an attitude of near-continual repentance all the way through? This is such a study.

Peter Hobson opens up key Christian truths in a way that reveals breathtaking new heights and dimensions of God's provision, especially in relation to our equipping against problems, those not caused by remnant fleshly bad habits or lack of positive confession, but rather through Satanic inroads.

Distributor

Mr. Stephen Banks, President
Impact Christian Books, Inc.
332 Leffingwell Ave., Suite 101
Kirkwood MO 63122
USA

Phone: (314) 822 3309   Fax: (314) 822 3325
Email: Stephen@impactchristianbooks.com
Website: www.IMPACTCHRISTIANBOOKS.com

International Contacts

Rev. Abraham Victor Babu
Abundant Grace Ministries
    Viravada, Pithapuram
    E. G. Dt 533450
    Andhrapradesh
    SOUTH INDIA
    Email:
    victorbabuad@rediffmail.com

Evang. Frank Williams Aboagye
    P. O. Box Se 2254
    Kumasi - Suame
    Ghana
    W. AFRICA
    Email:
    frankwilliamsaboagye@yahoo.com

Bishop Dr. P. Yeshaiah
Full Salvation Fellowship Of India
    #5-25-27B, J. P. Nagar
    Ithanagar
    Tenali 522 201
    A.P.
    SOUTH INDIA

Bishop Benwel Asiago
Full Salvation Ministry
    P. O. Box 3438, Kisii 40200
    Kenya,
    EAST AFRICA
    Phone: (254) 727 054 056
    Email: fsm_kenya2005@yahoo.com

PASTOR EMMANS WANG
The Prophetic Hill
  P. O. Box 4 Vom
  Jos
  Plateau State
  Nigeria
  W. AFRICA

EMAIL:
Emmanswang@yahoo.com

PASTOR GRACE OKURUT
Full Missions Ministry
  P. O. Box 584
  Soroti
  Uganda
  E. AFRICA

EMAIL:
okurutg@yahoo.com

PASTOR EMMANUEL SARFRAZ
  AFM Church
  Hali Public School
  Haji Pura
  Jamilabad Road
  Chungi No. 1
  Multan

PAKISTAN

EMAIL:
sadiqhali@Hotmail.Com

BISHOP ERNESTO BALILI
  265 Vamenta Blvd.
  Carmen
  Cagayan de Oro City
  PHILIPPINES

EMAIL:
bishopbalili@yahoo.com

PASTOR SURESH A. KOSHY
  132 Krishnappa Layout aji Pura
  Dodakanally, Sarjapura Road
  Karmalaram Post
  Bangalore 560035
  Karnataka State, INDIA

Impact Christian Books

These books are available through your local bookstore,
or you may order directly from
Impact Christian Books.

Website: www.impactchristianbooks.com

Phone Order Line: **1-800-451-2708**
(314)-822-3309

Address: **Impact Christian Books**
332 Leffingwell Ave. Suite #101
Kirkwood, MO 63122

- You may also request a Free Catalog -

Printed in Australia
AUOC02n0842301014
264039AU00010B/12/P